Graham was born in 1942 in NW London, the youngest of three. Family holidays were in UK until late teens when his first air trip overseas started the ball rolling. Following, he joined an airline at Heathrow in 1963 and worked there for 11 years before moving to Auckland, New Zealand, and worked with two further airlines for eight years before moving to Gold Coast Australia. Here he was involved in travel agency work from 1983 through to retirement in 2007 and continued travelling right through to 2020. This accounts for the varied destinations and countries he has visited in 59 years of travelling.

Firstly, I have to thank my wife, Anne, for being so patient during the hours I spent researching this book. With respect to my time in the aviation industry I think the writing of this book is in large part due to my huge regard to the professionalism of all involved in the operation of an airline.

I was privileged to be a small part of that for 19 years of my working life and would dedicate this book to the aircrews of British Airways, Air New Zealand and Pan American who I liaised with over those years of my working life.

Graham Hyslop

WHEN THE WEIGHT OF THE PAPER...

AUSTIN MACAULEY PUBLISHERS™
LONDON * CAMBRIDGE * NEW YORK * SHARJAH

Copyright © Graham Hyslop 2024

The right of Graham Hyslop to be identified as author of this work has been asserted by the author in accordance with sections 77 and 78 of the Copyright, Designs and Patents Act 1988.

All rights reserved. No part of this publication may be reproduced, stored in a retrieval system, or transmitted in any form or by any means, electronic, mechanical, photocopying, recording, or otherwise, without the prior permission of the publishers.

Any person who commits any unauthorised act in relation to this publication may be liable to criminal prosecution and civil claims for damages.

All of the events in this memoir are true to the best of author's memory. The views expressed in this memoir are solely those of the author.

A CIP catalogue record for this title is available from the British Library.

ISBN 9781398486201 (Paperback)
ISBN 9781398486218 (ePub e-book)

www.austinmacauley.co.uk

First Published 2024
Austin Macauley Publishers Ltd®
1 Canada Square
Canary Wharf
London
E14 5AA

I would like to thank a number of people in making this book possible, and especially the advice and help I've received from Flight Captains Richard de Crespigny, Jim McEnlly and Warwick Tainton. Also, photos and advice from my old BEA (British European airways) friend, Fred Barnes.

In addition, I'm grateful for photos included, taken by John Roach, Rob Finlayson, Howard Chaloner, David Carter, David Oates, Paul Seymour and also Boeing with the help of Stewart Wilson in including that photo. I'd also like to thank all my past work mates including the Panam ones in Auckland for filling in a few 'hazy' patches in the memory bank!

There are many others who were contacted to obtain information and I cannot thank you all individually, but I'd be very remiss if I did not mention my near neighbours, Karen and Jane, and brothers Ameritus, Prof. James Corkery and Martin for all their assistance and expertise in the area of book publishing which has helped me enormously.

A really big thank you!

Table of Contents

Prologue — 22
- *Aircraft Photos* — 22
- *Travel Photos* — 22
- *Sectors* — 23
- *New Types* — 23
- *Abbreviations* — 24
- *Heathrow* — 24
- *Flight Times* — 25
- *Historical Note* — 25

My Brief Life Story — 26

Now Let's Start Travelling! 1961 — 31
- *March to Geneva* — 31
- *Vickers Armstrong Viscount V802* — 31
- *De Havilland Comet 4B (DH106)* — 32
- *June To Paris Air Salon* — 34
- *Douglas DC-7C* — 34
- *August/September/December, Glasgow to London* — 36
- *Vickers Armstrong Vanguard V953* — 36

1962 — 38
- *This was a Year of Weddings in the Family.* — 38

June To Belfast	38
July	39
September, West Scotland Trip	39
Handley Page Hp44 Dart Herald	40
De Havilland Heron 1B (DH114)	41
December New Year in Prestwick	42
Boeing 707-465	**43**
1963	**45**
Joined BEA – February 11th	45
May Sikorsky S55 Flight	46
June to Paris Air Salon	47
Sud Aviation Caravelle 3 Se210	47
1964	**49**
January to the Scilly Isles	49
De Havilland DH89A Dragon Rapide	49
September To Lisbon	51
1965	**52**
January to Scotland	52
June to Europe	53
1966	**55**
February Operations Course	55
March to USA	55
Canadair CL44J	60
May Flight Planning	61
1967	**63**
September to Milan	63
Armstrong Whitworth Argosy AW650-222	64

1968	**65**
February to New Zealand	*65*
Fokker Friendship F27	*66*
Vickers Armstrong Super VC10	*68*
Sad Sequel to G-ARWE	**69**
April, Stockholm Famil:	*69*
June 1968 to January 1969 to Norway	*70*
Douglas DC9-40	*70*
Cessna 185 Skywagon	*71*
August to Bergen	*72*
Convair CV440 Metropolitan	*73*
1969	**75**
January to South America	*75*
Douglas DC8-33	*77*
Boeing 727-200	*78*
BAC111-500	*80*
April to Greenland	*81*
Sikorksky S61N	*84*
May to New Zealand	*85*
Boeing 720	*87*
Taking Stock	*88*
1970	**90**
Romance Number Three	*90*
July to Athens	*90*
Hawker Siddeley Trident 2E	*91*
1971	**93**
January to New Zealand	*93*

July to Faro Portugal	94
Proposal	94
October to Paris	95
1972	**96**
April	96
Hawker Siddeley Trident 3B	97
October to Crete	98
1973	**99**
March to Gibraltar	99
Moving from Heathrow?	99
July to Inverness	100
October, a Visit for Anne to See NZ	100
Boeing 747-136	101
Douglas DC10-30	102
Around Home	104
1974	**106**
March	106
August the Move to NZ!	106
Vickers Armstrong Standard VC10	107
Getting Started in NZ	108
1975	**110**
1976	**112**
June	112
July to UK	113
Lockheed L1011 Tristar	113
August to Hawkes Bay	114
Changes in NZ	115

December to Papeete	*115*
1977	**116**
1978	**117**
July to Sydney	*117*
Boeing 747SP	*117*
Boeing 747-100F	*119*
1979	**121**
March to Sydney	*121*
August to UK	*122*
1980	**123**
April to Sydney	*123*
August to Honolulu	*123*
Cessna 402A	*124*
Boeing 737-200	*125*
1981	**127**
June to UK	*127*
Boeing 747-238 Combi	*128*
Boeing 747-200	*129*
July	*130*
September to Sydney Fact Finding	*131*
Later September	*131*
October to Honolulu	*132*
November to Sydney More Fact Finding	*132*
1982	**134**
February to Sydney One Way!	*134*
1983	**136**
October, Travel Agency Opens	*136*

1984	**137**
1985 and 1986	**138**
1987	**139**
March to Sydney	*139*
April to Hamilton Island	*139*
December to Lady Elliott Island	*139*
Britten-Norman BN-2 Islander	*140*
1988	**142**
January	*142*
February	*144*
September to Sydney	*145*
Boeing 767-200	**145**
November to UK	*146*
1989	**148**
January	*148*
1990	**149**
February to Fiji	*149*
April to Solomons	*149*
De Havilland Canada DHC6 (Twin Otter)	*151*
October to Japan	*152*
December to NZ	*153*
1991	**154**
August to Hong Kong	*154*
Boeing 747-400	*154*
1992	**156**
March to Bali	*156*
Bae 146-300	*156*

April to Sydney	157
December to Melbourne/Snowy Mountains	158

1993   159

1994   160

March to Vanuatu	160
April	161
May to Sydney to Join a Cruise	161
June to Cairns	162
October to NZ	162
SAAB 340A	163
December to Japan	164

1995   166

May to Noumea	166
September via Hong Kong to Macau	167
November to Tasmania	168

1996   169

March to Sydney	169
May to Sydney	170
September to Bangkok	170
October to NZ	171

1997   172

March to NZ	172
Future Thoughts	173
September to Singapore	173
Airbus A300B4-200	174
October, A Big Day	175
November to Canberra	176

December *177*

1998 .... **178**

1999 .... **179**

February to Tasmania *179*

July to Scandinavia *179*

McDonnell Douglas MD80 .... *185*

Fokker F50 .... *186*

2000 .... **188**

September to Sydney for the Olympics *188*

2001 .... **189**

June to Sydney *189*

2002 .... **190**

February to NZ *190*

Embraer Bandeirante 110 .... *190*

2003 .... **192**

July to Cairns *192*

September to Cairns (Again) *193*

September to Singapore *193*

Boeing 777-200 .... *193*

2004 .... **195**

January to Melbourne *195*

May to Iceland *196*

Boeing 757-200 .... *198*

Dornier 228 .... *199*

October to Sydney *200*

2005 .... **201**

A Decision Time *201*

May to Canada/Alaska	*201*
Avro 748-2A	*205*
Airbus A320-200	*206*
October to Longreach	*207*
De Havilland Canada DHC Dash 8-200	*208*

2006 — 209
Christmas 2006	*209*

2007 — 211
May	*211*
November to South America/Antarctica	*211*
Airbus A340-200	*220*

2008 — 222
July to UK	*222*
Airbus A330-300	*226*
Airbus A319-100	*227*

2009 — 229
November to NZ	*229*

2010 — 230
June to Sydney	*230*

2011 — 231
March to Lady Elliot Island	*231*
Cessna 208b Grand Caravan	*232*
May a Flying Lesson!	*233*
Cessna 172R Skyhawk	*233*
September to NZ	*234*

2012 — 237
February Start with Care Flight	*237*

November to Cairns	*238*
2013	**240**
April to Northern Territory Eclipse Time Again!	*240*
2014	**245**
January	*245*
June to Sydney	*245*
November to NZ	*246*
2015	**249**
August to Adelaide	*249*
Sad News from New Zealand	*250*
August to NZ	*250*
December to Norway/UK	*251*
Boeing 787-8	*258*
Airbus A380-800	*259*
2016	**261**
Lifeflight	*261*
August to Cairns	*262*
November Gold Coast Airport Ambassador Programme Starts	*263*
2017	**266**
Anne's Friend	*266*
May to Europe	*266*
Embraer E190	*268*
Airbus A350-900	*269*
2018	**271**
July Local Helicopter Flight	*271*
August to Sydney	*272*
2019	**273**

January to NZ	*273*
March	*273*
August to Western Australia	*274*
October to Norway then Lower Europe	*275*
Bombardier CRJ900	*281*
Airbus A320NEO	*282*
Doctor's Report	*283*
2020	**284**
February to NZ	*284*
Travel Trivia	*286*
Glossary/General Information	**288**
General Information	*290*
Runway Directions	**291**
May 2022: A Postscript	**292**
Index	**294**

If you have been associated with aviation, the above book title will have a very good meaning to you and no doubt has brought a smile to your face! But for others who might need an explanation it follows here. Aviation thrives on a mountain of paperwork from manuals, performance charts, maintenance logs and the list goes on.

Many years ago, a gentleman by the name of Donald Wills Douglas came up with the quote: **"When the weight of the paper equals the weight of the airplane, only then you can go flying."**

Every airline has its own version of the saying, and the first airline I worked for back in the 1960s, it was "When the weight of the paper equals the weight of the airplane, you were good to go" but the essence of the quotation is the same.

Prologue

This book covers my life, especially the period from when I started to travel by air in 1961 until present, and anything of significance that happened during those years is included together with the accounts of the flying trips. From my early days until my first flight to Switzerland, I've outlined in a little more detail in "My Brief Life Story Segment".

Aircraft Photos

Photography has been a hobby of mine but having said that, sometimes the 64 aircraft types I required photos of, certainly some were at night and more recently from "gate" to "gate" not always lending itself to a good image.

If I could not get a good photo on the day, I've tried to get one on a later date, in some cases have been grateful for support from other aviation photographers who have been credited, and in others, have used a "sister ship" more so if there is an interesting aviation story attached to it.

Travel Photos

I've tried to be selective as to what's included in the Travel photos. I think a lot of folks have been to Paris and London so you won't find them here! I've always had a passion for cold weather countries and Arctic regions so there are plenty of Greenland, Spitzbergen, Falklands, Antarctica and the like, so hopefully this will give the book a greater appeal than having included too many mainstream destinations.

Even now living in Australia, I still manage to get to Northern Norway! At latest count the flight log totals 21 landings or take offs inside the Arctic circle!

Sectors

Over my years of flying, I have flown 454 sectors. Although, a few were just single sectors, the vast majority have been in multi sector trips to arrive at a total of 124 trips. However, in some instances there were some trips that were a little repetitive and these have not been included in the book.

Such examples would be, during my four years employed with Panam in Auckland, 6 round trips were made to Sydney, but 2 are not mentioned in the book. More relevant is since moving to Australia we have been in SE Queensland since 1982 and I have personally done 17 round trips to Sydney!

If they revolved around a big family occasion, they are mentioned but quite a number were one night Travel agent workshops where no new types were involved in the journey, so five trips have been left out on this route.

New Types

One never knows on an itinerary what aircraft types are going to show up along the way.

Once you have flown with your host airline a couple of times, it's normally when you get to fly with another airline for the odd sector that a new type enters the scene.

In my first round the world in 1968 it totalled 20 sectors but only two new types.

In following years, a 1969 round world was 15 sectors long with one new type, and in 1971 it totalled 17 sectors with no new types! Also, on the subject of new types where this occurs on a trip, I have kept its first mention as brief as possible (such as this is a new type see details below). I can assure readers, I have made every attempt to keep the information to the necessary but give you a fair account of the travel journeys.

In the notes regarding aircraft types in this book, this has to be fairly brief, so gives you some basic information. It is not an aviation textbook. There is a myriad of those around and many specialise just on a particular type and many make interesting reading.

This book is designed as a more general guide to reflect my travels, for those not only interested in aviation but also in travel. There are many travellers, I'm sure, who will pick up this book, and have never seen or heard of a Dragon Rapide outlined as my 21st flight in 1964! They just don't make them like that anymore, and it was a graceful sight to see one!

My notes on each type I trust will give you enough information to provide you an overall view of the plane. There are now so many variations especially in later years on airliner models, stretched versions, extended ranges etc., there was only room in this book for the brief details provided.

Abbreviations

In order to keep this book somewhat shorter, in some instances longer airline names such as Singapore Airlines, for the first time they were used in the book, have been provided with their two-letter prefix code which precedes their flight number. In this case, the code is SQ.

Once this has been given in the book, I think many who have a thirst for travel are familiar with most of the major airline codes, but if you need reminding when you see that code, later you will find it in the glossary at the end of the book. For some others with a shorter name, such as Qantas, I have just put the name in full each time.

The glossary/general information also gives a little background on the airlines where something needs to be explained and details some other information which I think will prove useful and is not generally known.

Heathrow

As per abbreviations, once this is first stated in full, it's reduced to LHR but as nearly all my flights were in and out of this port in London, to save putting that in to the point of monotony I have for variance included here and there the name "London" which always means Heathrow airport. If I ever use Luton, Gatwick or London City, it will clearly say so.

No, I didn't forget Stansted. It's one airport I haven't been through!

Flight Times

To break up the pattern in the book, occasionally I mention a flight time on a given flight.

It will give some readers an idea of distances travelled if you are unfamiliar with the sectors that have been flown.

Historical Note

By chance the last sector we flew was as recent as March 2nd, 2020, when Covid-19 was just beginning to be recognised to be a worldwide pandemic. Progressively during March, flights reduced worldwide until by April there had been an 80% reduction worldwide in aviation activity.

My notes regarding individual aircraft as to whether they were in storage or not are from information drawn from various sources as of mid-2021. Some of the newer types of planes have probably returned to flying, but in some cases, press releases have not caught up with these facts.

I ask readers to take this into account when reading the book. I have made every effort to make the information as accurate as I could possibly make it. Sadly, with the onset of Covid some older types and especially most of the 747's that should have gone on for a few more years came to a rather unexpected early end.

Whilst passenger aircraft are now returning to our skies, there has been a huge increase in cargo operations, especially with A350 and 787's carrying vaccines and PPE worldwide to combat the pandemic.

My Brief Life Story

679 Honeypot Lane, Stanmore
My birthplace in the UK

Fuller details will be embodied into my travel journey, so this is a brief summary mainly of the earlier years to give you an idea of my earlier upbringing and some of the holidays we did near home before my first overseas trips started.

I was born in the middle of the Second World War on May 27th, 1942, and as was the custom to keep hospitals free for more urgent cases, I was born at our home address of which there is photo included. We occupied the house just to the left of the centre archway and the block contained four dwellings.

The suburb is called Stanmore, about 10 miles NW of London which is in the borough of Harrow, and Winston Churchill was educated at the school on Harrow Hill.

After the war ended, although, I find this hard to believe because I have vivid memories of this at only the tender age of just over three; myself, my mum and dad, plus my brother, Stewart, aged seven years, and my sister, Elaine, aged five, headed off in our Standard car (practically the only car in the street at the time, see photo) for a camping holiday at Lulworth Cove in Dorset on the south coast of the UK (a recent photo including my wife is shown). The atmosphere at that camping holiday with the war only just ended can only be described as 'euphoric!'

Lulworth Cove. Taken on a winter break in the 1970s, back in 1945 scene of my first post-war holiday.

Standard Big 9 Car. Our family mode of transport for many of our Post war holidays. "Image created by Simon GP Geoghegan."

Later in 1949 when I was seven, we had a holiday at Dymchurch down in Kent and there is a family photo of me, complete with broken arm standing on the footplate of a loco of the narrow-gauge Romney Hythe Dymchurch railway, which still runs to this day. Also, at the same time most of the houses in our street were rented from the builder and so it was quite easy to do mutual swops so for whatever reason a family about five houses up the road wanted to move to our house so we moved to their semi-detached type dwelling.

After that in the early 50s, my father purchased a 15ft caravan which we towed with that tiny Standard car down to Bognor in West Sussex. How we never had an accident towing it beggars' belief. Nobody believed in towing weights then, and then there was the five of us in the car to start with!

Over a period of years, we moved it progressively west, next onto Barton-on-Sea near Bournemouth, and then finally to Brixham in Devon where we had several years of holidays. We later had a larger van over on the east coast near Harwich in Essex which I visited in my teen years.

By 1953, I'd gone from a primary school to two years at a secondary school and then moved to a Building Technical College some miles nearer to London, which involved a ride of around five stops on the London underground line that came out to our area. This was the same school my brother had attended ahead of me.

I left this college in 1958 with fairly good results and started working for a company called Dexion as a draughtsman. They manufacture steel slotted angle (a Meccano like product) which can be assembled into storage racks and other applications. I also was allowed to be released one day per week to return to college for a higher qualification, but Dexion and I parted ways before that happened.

In late 1962, Dexion suggested they wanted more turnover from me (frankly I'm a detail man) and I wasn't producing enough quotes for them.

I tried to step up for them but we both realised that my true heart lay elsewhere and I applied for jobs in the aviation industry. I applied for an Air Traffic Controller cadet position, and with BEA a job as an operations recorder in their operations department at Heathrow. I was successful in both of these applications but elected to join BEA, which I did so on February 11th, 1963.

I should now explain that during my teen years, my main hobby had been cycling away from my home to nearby airfields and airports and air shows (and further afield hitchhiking) was the order of the day! On one day cycling back from Heathrow (12 miles to the SW from my house), I managed to catch up with what turned out to be a fellow enthusiast name of Jeffery. After that we went everywhere together and am still in touch. A recent photo is shown.

Also at Heathrow, we met up with a group of aviation enthusiasts down from Prestwick airport in Scotland and I became firm friends with many of these, so some of these folk features in my later travels too. David, one of this group, relocated down to NW London to a suburb close to mine, so we became close friends for many years.

So, from mid-teens until around age 20, my main hobby would be aviation and photography travelling with the various friends outlined above.

Closer to home from my technical college days, I met up with Roger and am still in touch with him and we used to visit many pubs together and shared my first trip to Switzerland and the Lisbon trip of 1964.

From joining BEA in 1963, I was with them until officially March 31st, 1974 when they merged With BOAC (British Overseas Airways Corporation) to become BA (British Airways) and I was only with them until August of that year.

During the later years with BEA, on a 'Foggy day in London Town', I met for the first time with my wife to be, and we married in April 1972.

You'll see it's detailed in the travel notes, we emigrated to NZ (New Zealand) in 1974, and after a brief two weeks in a travel agency outside Auckland, AIR NZ (Air New Zealand), who originally could not offer me a vacancy came up with a position in flight deck rosters which I took up and in 1976, I moved down one floor in their downtown office building to flight control in a clerical position.

Panam then came up with Loadmaster positions at Auckland airport in September 1977, so I moved there and had four happy years until the airline started reducing staff and was laid off in September 1981.

Things were bleak in NZ for another aviation position at the time, so we moved to Australia, to the Gold Coast, and ran our own travel agency from October 1983 until October 1997.

After that, I sometimes worked fulltime but mainly part time at other travel agencies around the Gold coast until I retired in 2007.

In summary, other than a brief break after leaving Panam in September 1981 and opening our own travel agency here in Australia around two years later, I have been in the travel industry from February 1963 to October 2007, some forty-four and a half years!

Other airport activities since then have been volunteer work with Lifeflight, a helicopter and fixed wing medical rescue organisation, where I guided tours around their Gold Coast hanger from 2012 to 2016.

Then meet and greet as an ambassador, again at Gold Coast airport from 2016 to 2019.

Now Let's Start Travelling! 1961

March to Geneva

Roger, my pal from Building College days and myself decided on a holiday to Montreux in Switzerland. We booked through Thomas Cook holidays, one of the original tour operator companies (sadly no longer in operation). Stayed at Hotel de Londres in Montreux, later the setting for part of "Love and Bullets" movie.

Used a rail/bus ferry pass to great effect to see many parts of Switzerland including Zermatt and the Matterhorn and also Mt Blanc and Gstaad. Flight out and back were my first and second flights and different types so details are below. Lots of snow in late March and a great holiday!

Vickers Armstrong Viscount V802

This aircraft has been the most successful airliner produced by the British and in all 445 aircraft were built. It started in basic operations with the smaller 700 series aircraft in 1953 which was recognised by its oval type cabin doors compared with the later more rectangular style doors on the larger 800 series that followed.

BEA operated my first flight and registration was G-AOHM, and it was a night flight from LHR (Heathrow) to Geneva on March 27th, 1961.

The airline had taken delivery of the first 802 Viscounts in February, 1957 and HM the aircraft I flew on had its first flight on May 30th, 1957. It continued to fly with BEA/BA well into the 70s, then with many other operators until damaged during a take-off in Chad and written off in March 2001. Photo is showing sister ship OHJ on approach to Heathrow.

Viscounts continued to be delivered to various operators worldwide including the USA until the final 445th unit was delivered to China.

The Viscount and the Vanguard that followed both enjoyed really large windows and the Rolls Royce darts in the Viscount had a most glorious sound and powered many other airliners in the 1950s and 1960s. The Fokker Friendship, Avro 748 should be mentioned but there were many more.

Seating capacity on the 800's was around 60, in a 2-3 layout across the cabin.

In all I flew on seven Viscount flights but most were domestic flights within UK. There are two which are of more interest, which will be mentioned later in the book.

Vickers Viscount V802 March 1961. Shows another 802 G-AOHJ on approach LHR.

De Havilland Comet 4B (DH106)

The history of the Comet goes back to the Comet 1, which took to the skies July 27th, 1949 and it went into service with BOAC (British Overseas Airways Corporation) in the early 1950s, but sadly after several crashes revealed faults in the construction, which needed drastic revisions. The De Havilland company lost their big lead in the jet airliner business.

By the time their improved Comet 4's was ready and the first delivered to BOAC on September 30th, 1958, and they flew the first trans-Atlantic jet service, LHR to Idlewild (now JFK), on October 4th; it was only three weeks prior to Panam's 707 New York to Paris flight.

The 4B I returned from Geneva to Heathrow on was G-APMB. It had been delivered to BEA on November 9th, 1959 and my flight was April 4th, 1961.

This aircraft stayed with the BEA until 1970 when it was transferred to Channel airways, then to Dan air and withdrawn from use in December 1978. The photo shown is sister ship PMF arriving at Lisbon in September 1964.

The 4B was made into a shorter haul version compared to the 4C which had two pinion tanks on the wing for longer range. The 4B had a two metre longer fuselage and shorter wingspan but still had a good range and tended to be used for the longer BEA routes such as London to Moscow, Tel Aviv etc. A total of 114 Comet units were built, and of these, 20 were 4B's, 18 for BEA and two for Olympic Airways. Seating on BEA's Comet 4B's was for 99 passengers.

I flew on four Comet sectors in all. Last Comet retired from service was a 4C in March, 1997. There are six aircraft in various museums located in UK, Germany and USA.

It should also be mentioned the Royal Air Force needed a replacement aircraft to perform Maritime Patrol duties, and they selected the Comet airframe and it was heavily modified into the very successful Nimrod aircraft of which 51 were constructed and served with great success.

It might be of interest here to compare my first two flights as one was a turboprop and the second, a jet. Within Europe sometimes the distances are not that great (London and Geneva are 462 miles apart). The flight out on the Viscount was 1hr 49 mins. Flight time going back on the Comet was 1hr 15mins.

When you got to deal with London to Paris, Brussels or Amsterdam it virtually made no difference at all! However, the appeal of flying in a jet had an obvious appeal for the public, but the economics for the airlines of the slightly slower turboprops on short routes was undeniable.

De Havilland Comet 4B April 1961. Shown is G-APMF at Lisbon September 1964.

June To Paris Air Salon

This trip staying at a small hotel in a side street around corner from Place du Republique. A trip with Jeffrey and Mike from the LHR crowd. Not sure how everyone had travelled over but I was the only one on the BOAC flight.

Only two full days there, one racing around various small airfields to the south of Paris, and then the Sunday at LeBourget to see the Air show. So, the DC7C was an unexpected type to fly on this route and the details are below.

Douglas DC-7C

This aircraft from Douglas preceded by the DC4 from the 1940s then later the DC6.

Ultimately, became one of the final prop type airliners before the advent of the jets in the late 1950s. Its other competitors were the Lockheed Constellation and the Boeing Stratocruiser

The DC-7C was introduced in 1956 and the plane I flew on registration G-AOIE was delivered to BOAC (British Overseas Airways Corporation) on December 14th, 1956. My first of two flights was LHR to Le Bourget to view the Paris Air Salon on June 2nd, 1961. Due to Le Bourget, then being closed over the weekend to passenger flights the return flight to London was from Paris Orly on June 5th, 1961.

After use by BOAC, it passed through several operators until put into storage in 1982. In all 121 DC-7C were built.

I had been expecting to travel on a newly introduced BEA Vanguard but found when we were bussed to an outer stand, this BOAC aircraft waiting for us. Due to the high number of aviation enthusiasts wanting to travel to the air show, BEA who operated the route had brought in extra flights, although, the flight number (BE364) didn't indicate anything out of the ordinary. Often extra flights have four-digit flight numbers or some other way of identifying them.

Most of our group made a rush to the front cabin which normally is first class with BOAC. Why they put first class here alongside those four powerful noisy engines is anybody's guess. In BEA Vanguards when they carried First it was down the back as far from the engines as possible. Photo below is "OIE" taken at BOAC maintenance area Heathrow.

This aircraft had operated a royal flight for Queen Elizabeth 2nd from Heathrow to Idlewild New York and a plaque on the rear of the cockpit bulkhead had the details.

Douglas DC-7C June 1961. Aircraft at later date in BOAC maintenance area Heathrow.

35

August/September/December, Glasgow to London

My first romance section!

All of these trips were Glasgow to London from the old Renfrew airport right up to January 1963 to visit a girlfriend, name of Kathy, who lived in Glasgow. Whilst I was working for Dexion in Kilburn London, staff from the Glasgow office and their relatives, down for a trip had visited our office and I had met Kathy. This was worth a 400-mile trip to Glasgow, so in all cases I travelled up by surface but flew back!

The August, flight was a further Viscount sector. Then September 29th was my first Vickers Vanguard flight (see details below), and then there were four more southbound Vanguard sectors through to January 1963.

More romance to follow!

Vickers Armstrong Vanguard V953

This aircraft was their 900-series airplane, as such used a lot of experience from their predecessor the successful Viscount. I never flew on its western competitor which was basically the Lockheed Electra but the Vanguard sold poorly, building only 44 aircraft selling only to BEA and TCA (Trans Canada Airlines) compared to the Electra which had built 170 units. I had ten flights in Vanguards and thought it was an excellent type with a high cruising speed of over 400 mph.

First delivery to BEA was on December 17th, 1960. The Vanguard I flew on G-APEJ was delivered on August 16th, 1961 and my flight was only two days later on the 18th from Renfrew airport Glasgow to LHR. After serving with BEA/BA into the mid-1970s, it went to other operators as a freighter until retirement in 1992.

Again, this had the large oval windows like the earlier Viscount. This time for a much larger airliner carrying 139 passengers the power units were Rolls Royce Tynes of around 4500 shp (shaft horse power). They were used in the CL44's and other types also. The aircraft also featured inbuilt air stairs.

In BEA's fleet of 20, there were six 951's models and fourteen 953's. The 953 had a higher take-off weight by around three tonnes at around 64.5 tonnes.

In 1969, nine of these were converted to become BEA freighters called Merchantman with a cargo loading door on the forward left side. Other aircraft remaining in the fleet stayed operating into the 1970s, but all were eventually sold off to other passenger or freight operators.

Of the ten Vanguard sectors, I've flown eight which are covered in these pages from September, 1961 to January, 1963. The remaining two will be mentioned later in the book.

Shown below is "EB" the second V951 in the fleet at LHR in the 1960s.

One Vanguard G-APEP a 953 was donated to Brooklands Museum in October 1996 and is displayed there.

Vickers Vanguard V953 September 1961. Shows G-APEB a V951 being positioned at LHR.

1962

This was a Year of Weddings in the Family.

Firstly, my brother who had returned from his army service in Singapore and North Borneo in surveying work, joined Hunting Aero Surveys at Boreham Wood, NW of London, close to the Elstree film studios. There he met Brenda, his wife to be, and I was honoured to be Stewart's best man at their wedding in March 1962.

By the following year, they had headed off to NZ to seek better fortunes there. At that time, especially for my parents, although, the jet age was upon us, it seemed a bridge too far to think they would ever see them again, but our later story relates a totally different tale.

June To Belfast

Next, I was invited to be best man at my cousin Alan's wedding at Ballymena in Northern Ireland, so flew up on a Saturday, June 9th in another BEA Vanguard, attended the wedding at Ballymena church, then moved onto a reception at a lovely spot at a NE coastal village, overlooking the water towards Scotland's Mull of Kintyre where I would land in my next type later in the year. After spending an overnight, I flew to Glasgow on the Sunday to visit Kathy and spend one night there, then home to London in a further Vanguard flight.

However, regarding the Belfast to Glasgow sector there is a bit of a story some of it with a sad sequel.

I had been hoping to fly on a DC3 which had been the type on the winter schedules but come the summer, it had been changed to a Viscount and then lo and behold over the weekends it had been upgraded to a Vanguard! The aircraft was G-APEE, and sadly just over three years later, this plane was lost in a tragic crash in October, 1965 at LHR on a foggy night.

The flight had been a late-night operation from Edinburgh but on arrival LHR, it performed 2 overshoots (another term is go-arounds) due the crew not able to see the runway lights at minimum decision height. The crew attempted a third landing but due to many factors explained in the accident report the aircraft did not achieve a positive rate of climb and descended into the runway. The plane had a fairly light load that night but all 30 passengers plus six crew perished. After this event BEA ruled that after two attempts at landing crew must divert to an alternate airport.

July

My sister, Elaine, ties the knot with her fiancé, Brian. They had known each other for many years attending the same church, so shared the same beliefs and had strong bonds. Our respective homes had been fairly close to each other in NW London but when they married, they purchased a new bungalow (single story dwelling) at Dunstable which is 28 miles NW of London.

They are grateful to this day for something I said when they had an option of two properties in the street. They were number 7 and number 11. Number 7 looked up a short cul de sac opposite, and had views of the Dunstable downs beyond the end of the close, whereas number 11 just looked out to the opposite dwelling. The real estate guy said buy number 11 because you don't want headlights shining in through your windows, of cars coming down the cul de sac!

How many headlights are you going to see coming out of a small close at night? He knew he could sell number 7 at the drop of a hat and wanted to offload number 11 onto them! They bought number 7 and have been eternally grateful!

They send me sunset photos from time to time! And this is fifty-nine years on and they are still there. Changes have been made and it has an upstairs conversion now.

September, West Scotland Trip

I wanted to see some of the scenery in the west of Scotland, so headed north by surface and then flew on a Dart Herald (a new type so see details below) from Renfrew Airport Glasgow to Machrihanish airport on the Mull of Kintyre which serves nearby Cambeltown. From there on, a brisk sunny autumn day, I hitch hiked and bussed up to the west coast town of Oban for a one night stay.

Following day went out by Caledonian MacBrayne steamer to the delightful village of Tobermorey with its colourful waterfront buildings on the Island of Mull, again for one night. Next day, the steamer took me on to Castle bay the town on Barra at the southern end of the Outer Hebrides (now Called the Western Isles). However, the stop on the way at Tiree at the Inner Hebrides was longer, as the skipper went ashore to attend a friend's funeral.

Island time operates everywhere in the world! I had one night in the town at Barra at a B and B, and next day took a bus up towards the north end of the island where the flights from Glasgow land on the beach when tidal conditions are right.

The flight was due at noon but heard it was to run late due to tides, so tradition at that time was if you wanted a lunch, call in at a house and ask for a meal, and leave a little cash (if they would take it in return).

In due course, the flight operating with De Havilland Heron (again a new type so see details below) took off for Glasgow at 3.30PM, some 3hrs late purely due to tides not allowing the scheduled timing, I then had three more nights in Glasgow before heading back south to London on another of my ten Vanguard flights.

Handley Page Hp44 Dart Herald

This aircraft was one of many contenders in the late 1950s to be considered on the market as a DC3 replacement. I think the clear winner was the Fokker Friendship, but the Avro 748 was also in the market. Originally, the Herald flew in 1956 with four piston engines but they re-engined it to be powered by two Rolls Royce darts which brought it into line with the other types. However, only 44 Dart Heralds were built.

The aircraft I flew on G-APWC was delivered to BEA on April 30th, 1962 and I flew on it later that year on September 17th from Renfrew airport Glasgow to Machrihanish airport, serving Campbeltown on Mull of Kintyre. This was only a 58 mile hop lasting 25mins!

There were three Heralds operated by BEA on their Island routes and they carried 44 passengers, and were used until October, 1966 when replaced by Viscounts and the planes were sold to Autair another British airline of the time.

Photo shows the aircraft after arrival at Machrihanish. Apologies for the quality! PWC went eventually to Colombia and ceased operating there in the early 1980s.

PWA, a sister ship, is in a flight museum at Woodley near Reading where the aircraft were originally built.

Handley Page HP44 Dart Herald September, 1962. On arrival Machrihanish. Apologies for quality!

De Havilland Heron 1B (DH114)

This aircraft type was first flown from De Havilland's main airfield at Hatfield, north of London in May, 1950. BEA purchased two to fly on the Scottish Islands and highlands routes and to be used in Air ambulance work. The plane I flew on G-ANXA was delivered December 3rd, 1954. A third aircraft was added to the fleet in 1956, but sadly crashed on an emergency mission two years later, killing the two pilots and nurse on-board.

My flight on NXA was from Barra beach in the Outer Hebrides to Renfrew airport Glasgow on September 20th, 1962. Photo below shows plane on sand at Barra prior to departure. This aircraft was named Sister Jean Kennedy, after the nursing sister who had died in the 1958 rescue mission trying to land in bad weather on Islay.

The aircraft had no taxy time at Barra. Capt Barclay just rotated on the stand towards the open water and opened the throttles having every intention of getting airborne before we ran out of sand! Later you'll see I did this flight in reverse direction in 2008 in a Twin Otter not without a degree of excitement.

After arrival in Glasgow, aircraft was hosed down to remove any corrosive seawater.

This Heron was retired from service by BEA in 1973 and after flying with several other operators, was written off in NZ in 1981.

Typical passengers carried were 17 but this varied on the airline and 149 units were built, and a curious thing is that in the cabin you had to step over the wing spar going forward to the front of the plane. Later in life, many of these aircraft were re-engined with four Lycoming engines and the Saunders Company stretched the plane to carry 23 passengers and re-engined it with two Pratt and Whitney 750 shp turboprop engines.

There are many survivors of this type in numerous museums throughout the world.

De Havilland Heron 1B September 1962.
Prior departure from Barra.

December New Year in Prestwick

It was very snowy around Christmas time in London that year, and after several tries at getting out on BEA Vanguards to Renfrew, I bought a ticket to fly with BOAC on their flight that routes via Prestwick (an airport 30 miles SW of Glasgow) to New York. By then on December 28th, when I boarded my first 707 flight (see details below), I think the worst of the snow had gone, but in any event, I noted on my flight sheet "snowy day".

We departed from the gate only 10mins late. The idea of the trip was to spend New Year with my Prestwick friends and I stayed at David's house for the five nights and went back from Renfrew to London on January 2nd, in a further Vanguard, and to be honest half expected to be diverted. It was a really snowy night with strong crosswinds on the runways at LHR!

Boeing 707-465

The Boeing 707 first flew in December 20th, 1957 and had initially relied heavily on their military designs such as the B47 plus painful lessons learnt from the De Havilland Comet 1 crashes. So, this 400 series was a well-developed aircraft compared to the first 100 series aircraft that had entered trans-Atlantic service with Panam in October 1958.

The plane I flew on was G-ARWD which first flew on February 16th, 1961, and started flying with BOAC September 1962. I travelled on it LHR to Prestwick Airport in Scotland on December 28th, 1962. Flight time was 60mins and distance was 348 miles and cruise was at 32000ft! This aircraft carried on flying with BOAC then mainly in the BA family until scrapped in 1981.

865 Boeing 707 units were built and 154 of the B720 a shorter lighter variant.

Interestingly, this plane and its sister ship, G-ARWE, were model-465's, both delivered to Cunard Eagle in their colours in early 1962 and later in the year became part of the larger BOAC fleet of 436 models.

It seemed curious to me that despite RWD and RWE making up only two of BOAC's larger fleet of 707's, I seemed to meet up with them where ever I travelled. Of the total 36 sectors on 707's I flew, 29 were on BOAC and 14 of them were either on RWD or RWE! The other seven sectors were with Varig or TWA.

The photo shown is of RWE which suffered a sad fate and some loss of life. It was taken on the apron in Rangoon (now called Yangon) on February 12th, 1968.

I'll recall the full story later in the book.

There are many 707's in museums throughout the world.

Boeing 707-465 LHR-Prestwick December 1962. Taken of the other BOAC sister Ship G-ARWE on Rangoon apron in February 1968.

1963

Joined BEA – February 11th

Well, my interview previously had gone well with BEA! I don't think anyone else previously had sat in my chair and had the knowledge of their airline that I told them. Their eyebrows certainly were raised!

On day 1 when I joined BEA, it was in the position of an operations recorder. Looking back into the 1960s it was all analogue and the operations centre for BEA was a two-storey facility in the centre of what was the Queens building since demolished and replaced by new structures.

It was rather like an Ocean liners Atrium. On one side, the lower ground floor had a flight enquiries department and an upper gallery above them had the Fleet Controllers and assistants, and VHF (very high frequency) radio which all faced on the other side of the two-storey atrium a board, showing all the LHR operations for the airline.

The lower floor of the board opposite flight enquiries showed arrivals into LHR as that is what they generally dealt with. The upper part of the board showed departures opposite where the controllers sat, but by looking down they could also view the arrivals. Behind these boards was where I initially worked.

The boards displayed the full schedule for the day with STD (scheduled time of departure) for the flight and all the other relevant information for that flight. Aircraft type/registration was shown and booked passenger load. All of this was loaded onto the screen by small metal tags which slid through the board and resembled a very close louvre screen.

When it came to a departure if the STD was, say 1000, and we had a message say it departed the gate (sometimes called the ramp or blocks) at, say 1005, two tags would be slid through the louvres so all in front of the board could see +5. So basic but it worked!

I was at the back for probably eighteen months or so, then came around to the balcony and worked as an arrivals or departures assistant, assisting the

Controllers and on arrivals passing onto various departments on the airport, VHF radio messages passed to us by incoming flights which might include details of wheelchair passengers, maintenance issues etc. I stayed on the balcony until early 1966 but I'll reserve that part of the story until later.

May Sikorsky S55 Flight

This is a general-purpose helicopter and a great number of versions were used by military forces. It was not designed as such for passenger work but could carry ten people. BEA had several helicopters in their fleet in the early 60s and this was the one S55 they had and was built in 1954. First flight of the S55 was November 10th, 1949 and overall 1728 units have been built.

I was attending the Biggin Hill Air show (famous airfield for its role in WW2 days SE of London) and Capt. Prichard who I think knew I worked for BEA got me aside and got me a spare seat for a five-minute ride and the date was May 3rd, 1963. Photo below is yours truly posing with the aircraft!

It featured in several films including the Beatles film "A Hard Day's Night" in 1964.

This machine was used by other operators from 1969 and is in a Helicopter Museum at Weston Super Mare UK.

Sikorksky S55 Helicopter, Biggin Hill, May 1963.

June to Paris Air Salon

David and myself travelled over LHR to Paris (Orly Airport) on an Air France flight (details below). We waited there for Gordon and Stewart (two of the Prestwick crowd) who arrived shortly after on an Olympic one which operated LHR-Orly-Athens. It could carry passengers London-Paris under what is called Fifth freedom rights (see glossary).

Once we had all met up, I hired a VW from a hire car company in Paris and we toured around the French countryside in all directions from Paris but usually not more than 60 miles away. We attended the Air salon on the weekend dates and I was there for nine nights. The others did different itineraries after the show. I returned to London on the Olympic flight coming in from Athens operated by a Comet 4B.

Sud Aviation Caravelle 3 Se210

This aircraft was one of the first short to medium haul jet aircraft into the skies. It first flew on May 27th, 1955, and entered service with SAS (Scandinavian Airlines System) April 26th, 1959.

F-BJTM was the Air France Caravelle which I flew on and its first flight occurred on March 13th, 1963 and my flight from Heathrow to Paris Orly was just a few months later on June 8th, to visit the Paris Air Salon for my second time. This aircraft continued flying with Air France until 1975 when it went to Air Burundi and later went into storage.

This mark of Caravelle carried up to 99 passengers but later variants were stretched and carried up to 116. In all 282 were built. They were popular and were used by many airlines worldwide.

One curious thing I noticed when on-board was the positioning of the windows which either suited Frenchman who are maybe shorter or something else was wrong with how the windows had been positioned. Admittedly, I'm fairly tall at over 6ft but one would expect when sat in an airplane seat to be able to see out through the window.

The Caravelle had a teardrop shaped window which rose to a rounded peak at the top. That was the level of my eye so to achieve a view out of the window I had to hunch down in the seat to see anything. A very odd situation indeed.

I flew on six Caravelle sectors all within Europe, the five others being, one London-Lisbon, a London-Madrid and three others with SAS. Photo below is of an Air France sister ship taxiing at LHR.

There are several planes exhibited in museums around the world.

Sud Aviation Caravelle 3. June 1963. Of sister ship taxiing at LHR.

1964

January to the Scilly Isles

This is a beautiful part of the UK and enjoys a much better climate than many other parts of the country. My main reason for the visit was to get a ride on a Dragon Rapide whilst they were still in service! I stayed several nights in Penzance first, which is a lovely spot in its own right and close by is NewLyn harbour which has been portrayed by many an artist!

Also, just out from Penzance is St Michaels mount which you can gain access to at low tide! On January 15th, after a lovely 6 mile drive out to St Just airport close to Lands' End, I took the flight out to the Scillies. I spent six nights over on the Scilly isles and got to access most of the inhabited islands.

During my stay, I visited some of the green houses where they grow the daffodils that are shipped up to London's Covent Garden market. The aroma when you enter one of those buildings is absolutely amazing! After my stay, I returned to the mainland on the steamer, the 'Scillonia', and then by train from Penzance to London.

Other than the few inhabited islands there are a huge number of low-lying ones making up a very attractive scenic area and it's definitely a place everyone should try to visit!

De Havilland DH89A Dragon Rapide

This biplane type first flew in April 1934 and could carry eight passengers and was used as a short haul airliner in those early aviation days. 728 Rapides in all were built, but only around half of those were built by the middle of WW2, equally by De Havilland and at the Brush Coach works Loughborough the particular plane I flew on built at the latter and first flown in 1944.

As such it would have originally been known as a Dominie by the RAF (Royal Air Force) and received the registration NF851 and would have served as either a navigation trainer or in a communications role.

After the war, many surplus machines were then turned over to the civilian market and eventually BEA became the operator of this plane. This would be the only aircraft I've flown on that had a wartime history! At the time of my flight, it was just on 20 years old.

My flight on G-AJCL was on January 15th, 1964 from St Just (Lands' End Airport) in Cornwall UK, some 31 miles out to the Scilly Isles. Flight time just 13mins! BEA stopped running the Rapides shortly after this on May 2nd, 1964 and started flying Sikorsky S61 helicopters from nearby Penzance to the Scillies (see flight 94 in April 1969 for a similar S61N).

Photo below taken on morning of departure from St Just airport.

The Dragon Rapides that were surplus to BEA's needs were taken up by Scillonia Airways and they operated these aircraft from 1966 to 1969 Newquay-Penzance-Scillies.

There are still nine airworthy Rapides in the UK plus some in other countries many giving pleasure flights. Also, there are many more as exhibits in museums in a host of countries around the world.

Interestingly enough during a period of 2020 during the COVID pandemic the Lands' End to Scillies air Route was the busiest in the UK!

De Havilland Dragon Rapide January 1964. Prior to departure.

September To Lisbon

This was a second trip for me with Roger, my pal from college days. For some reason, I travelled earlier than he did. It might have been because of the days he could get off, or of different ticket conditions we had to comply with.

However, on my flight after we had reached TOC (Top of Climb) which heading from LHR to Lisbon would be somewhere over the Channel Isles (southern side of the English Channel), I experienced really severe sinus pains which just wouldn't go away. They persisted until we descended and landed in Lisbon. I've never had them again.

However, it did decide me to make this return journey by surface. I met Roger off his Comet 4B (the photo I used earlier) and we enjoyed a great holiday of around eight days. We also met up with two other people from BEA out there at the time so it was a good group.

On my last day and to partly minimise my journey home, Roger and I together with my bags headed NW to the very pretty fishing village of Nazare on the Atlantic coast. The WCs on the train were the type you don't do it in the station if you get my drift! Anyway, after a great day in Nazare, I headed east to Fatima and got a room for the evening in preparation to get the train coming up from Lisbon at about 1.30 AM heading towards Paris.

I was expecting something a bit flash with a dining car. There was nothing, just compartments and a corridor! Then next stop, about 60 contract workers got on going to a job in Beauvais, north of Paris. It then seemed the train was quite busy but the good news was they had brought all their goodies with them!

So, it wasn't long before I was feasting on bread and Pate, and I found the hooks in the cabin are not for hanging coats but rather their wine sacs, and they got me rather expert at using them! (The wine sacs that is!). That was the highlight of the journey.

Spanish rail at the time was click clack (pretty slow in other words). It took the whole day to go across Spain and then only about 6hrs from the border into Paris! After that I changed stations to Gare du Nord for a train up to Calais then a ferry to Dover.

A great holiday and a very memorable journey home!

1965

January to Scotland

This started with a northbound Vanguard flight on January 21st over a very snowy England up to Glasgow where I hired a VW, picked up two friends over in Edinburgh who rode with me for the day, and I dropped them off at Pitlochry station in the evening and they returned to Edinburgh by train.

Around 3 PM each day, I looked through my B and B guide to look for a possible place to stay, and when I fronted up, they basically said they weren't really open but made me welcome anyway. The sun was down by 4 PM at that time of the year.

The remainder of the month was spent travelling around the top end of Scotland in remarkably clear weather although very cold most days, and came over Applecross pass in west Scotland on January 30th one of the highest passes in the UK at 2054ft on a bright clear morning, which down in London was the funeral service of Sir Winston Churchill.

After this date, I still toured the Isle of Skye visiting Elgol (which I mention again later in the book) and have included a winter time view of the Black Cuillins from Elgol, before working my way back down to Glasgow to return the hire car, so though I don't have a date for the end of the trip it must have been eighteen days before I travelled back down to London by surface in first part of February.

A view of the Black Cuillins from Elgol in the Isle of Skye in January 1965.

June to Europe

This was the start of a seventeen-nights trip to Europe first visiting the Paris Air Salon but I didn't do any air sectors on this trip. I departed Victoria Station London on June 3rd by train to Folkstone then ferry to Boulogne and train into Paris.

I had met a young lady on the journey over, name of Sheila and I spent some time with her in Paris. She was living in London but was from Chile and visited her later there in 1969. So, we saw some sights together in Paris including artists in Montmartre etc. but then I did have to get down to the serious stuff of aviation, so met up with David and Stewart who had flown over.

We attended the Air Salon then travelled on with David by train to visit Basle, Zurich, Liechtenstein before arriving in Innsbruck. We stayed at a delightful Tyrolean village above Innsbruck called Igls. By the time we had arrived in Igls it was middle of following week since I had left London, and I enjoyed a ten night stay there.

David decided he wanted to see the Munich "scene" but way too early for Octoberfest! So, he departed a couple of days earlier from Igls. I then headed back after my ten-night stay via sleeper train and ferry again Boulogne to Folkstone arriving back into UK on Sunday, June 20th.

The Tyrolean valleys in June are a beautiful place to be with spring just having finished, plenty of snow still there, but magnificent fresh green foliage everywhere. Having said that see my comments later in February 1969 when I revisited in Winter. These places have scenic appeal in spades!

1966

February Operations Course

In due course of working with BEA, the next progression was to attend an operations course which was held at their training facility just to the NE of LHR at nearby Heston. I attended this together with some of my colleagues from operations at the airport plus BEA at Berlin and some employees of Iraqi airways who were operating Tridents similar to those in the BEA fleet.

We studied subjects such as Flight planning, Navigation, meteorology, aircraft performance and then there was an exam at the end of this course. The final exam was on Friday, March 25th. Assuming I had passed, on my return from the USA where I was departing to the next day, I would be assigned a place in the Flight Planning department.

March to USA

26 March I departed on BEA Trident 1, LHR to Brussels then from Luxembourg via Keflavik in Iceland to JFK, the last two sectors on a Canadair CL44J. Both of these were new types so details are in the text at foot of this portion!

Obtaining a visa to the US wasn't that easy then. I can recall making at least two visits to the US embassy in London to get the visa. How easy these days under the visa waiver programme for most visits! (See VWP in the glossary). I had lots of friends in North America plus two second cousins in the New York area (one named Alice in Manhattan), so was very fortunate in either having people to stay with or wanting to show me round.

When I arrived in New York, Alice gave up her apartment for my one week stay there. It was on the south side of W24th St with windows facing north and had a great view of the upper part of the Empire State building. On later visits during a summer thunderstorm, I've seen the spire on the top being struck by lightning at least a dozen times, truly a spectacular sight!

As an overseas visitor, I had access to a Greyhound bus pass which for ninety-nine days was $99! As well as seeing and being shown the sights of the "Big Apple" in the first week, I did a trial trip down to Philadelphia (a two-hour trip) to try out the pass. The daughter of one of the Iraqi Airways students on the course was living there so I called in and said hi!

At the end of my first week, I headed south proper with first stop Washington DC seeing the sights, some of them together with a friend I had met in London who lived near Washington. My stay there was with a friend of mine from the same street I lived in back home who now lived in a nearby suburb close to DC. Now I travelled further south to Daytona Beach in Florida then west to New Orleans.

Sadly, I wasn't too well there so didn't get to do everything I wanted to do. Then checking-in to head west with Greyhound the agent pointed out my pass had not been validated, so he looked at my passport and then based on that put an expiry date on the pass.

However, when I looked at it, it read 6/5/66, so I went back and said, "I will still be here until at least May 10th and you have put May 6th?"

He pointed to the 6 and said, "That's the month and that five is the date DUMMY!" I think his skill in dealing with customers needed some fine tuning but anyway, suitably corrected, as I was not aware of the American date system, I boarded the bus and headed west. Mid-morning, we stopped at Lake Charles and I was getting off the bus to have a drink during the short break and a man blocked my exit.

Can't remember if he even provided ID but he needed to see mine and asked to see my passport and checked me out and had obviously been asked by Greyhound at New Orleans to give me the once over! What a shame they haven't been as efficient in more recent years! I reached El Paso and went across the border into Mexico and in my naivety expected to see a sleepy village! That's one illusion busted!

On further west to Flagstaff from where I did a daytrip to the Grand Canyon. It's certainly Grand but not all times of the day do it justice. I hope my evening shot is better than the average.

On west to San Francisco where I had a friend of Alice's to show me round, and I've been fortunate to visit there again a number of times. Also, I think some friends from BEA, Connie and Margaret who now worked for an American Airline were rather surprised to see me! After that I went up the west coast to Tacoma south of Seattle (the airport serves both cities and is called SeaTac).

I had friends there to show me round and then up to Vancouver where again friends showed me some of it and I explored some of it on my own. Then east on the bus through the Rockies and I favour a road trip to see the best of this area. Even the bus will stop at scenic points but a hire car gives you even better freedom.

The rail whilst it's very luxurious does have limited stops so to be honest I don't think gives to you the best experience. Very late in the evening the bus arrives in Calgary where I am met by friends from the UK who moved out here. That was a Friday night, so next day, I hired a car and retraced a little back to Banff in the Rockies and saw all the sights around there including Lake Louise and the Columbian Icefield Highway and the Athabasca glacier.

After the weekend, I headed eastwards again through great sounding places like Medicine Hat and Moose Jaw to arrive in Winnipeg. I was to visit Andrea a friend of my sisters but she worked up north in the Lake Winnipeg Area. Around late April, this is the season called 'breakup' when ice is melting but the lakes are not free of ice, so flights cannot land on skis anymore and water is not sufficiently free of ice for floatplanes to land.

All I could do was say hi on the phone and headed to the airport and watched planes for the day! Then headed SE to Chicago where I saw the sights, then I spent some time out at O'Hare airport and made some good friends in United operations.

The Grand Canyon from the south rim in Arizona in evening sun. April 1966.

Heading east following the south shore of the Great lakes I arrived into Buffalo which is where Jimmy and Sally our parents' friends were now living. They and their two children (same names) were the ones we followed down to the south coast of England in the post war years in their little Austin "Box saloon". Jimmy and Sally senior took me up to Niagara Falls while I was staying with them and again, I revisited the falls on my trip up to Toronto.

I did have a friend there but wasn't able to get in touch, but enjoyed seeing the sights. Then following on the Canada side of the St Lawrence River NE and arrived at Montreal where I stayed with John who had been a fellow student at technical college. After seeing the sights with him and his girlfriend I travelled overnight south, back to New York on May 4th.

Well, I was just coming up to my 24th birthday but when I say of the thirty days I spent travelling around the USA, I spent twenty nights on overnight buses, it doesn't sound surprising in hindsight that I was totally exhausted. I wasn't in the frame of mind to go back via Keflavik and Luxembourg, so went into BA's office and bought myself a non-stop ticket to LHR!

I then had a further six nights in New York where Alice and her sister Bettie who lived out of the city showed me more sights. Certainly, New York in early

May was a very pleasant place compared to the very chilly place it was in late March when I arrived.

On May 10th, I left JFK on a BOAC 707-436 and with the help of a good Jetstream on that day covered the distance to LHR in 5hrs 47mins my best of four eastbound crossings I've made on that sector.

HAWKER Siddeley Trident 1C HS121

This aircraft built at De Havilland's Hatfield plant was originally to compete with the Boeing 727, but due to requests from BEA a shorter-range version than Boeing were marketing, was produced by DeHavilland and named the Trident.

In fullness of time, the Trident finally grew to a Trident 3B, roughly the size of a Boeing 727-200, but by then the bottom line was 117 Tridents had been built compared to over 1800 Boeing 727's! But the size of the respective aircraft doesn't tell the full story.

Originally, the 727-100 was a relatively short aircraft not that much different to the Trident 1 but major difference was that the Trident had been virtually made as a short haul airliner and the 727-100 by contrast whilst it carried only a few more passengers than the Trident 1, it could carry them over double the distance (2250 nautical miles nmi) and could therefore, be termed a medium haul airplane.

The 727 when it was stretched to the 200 model it was about the same size as a Trident 3B but with an impressive range of 2550 nmi, compared with around 1100 for the Trident 3B. Clearly, airlines made their choice as to which to purchase and the sales figures are the results.

The Trident 1 first flew on January 9th, 1962 and went into service with BEA April 1st, 1964.

G-ARPJ first flew on January 5th, 1964 and my flight LHR to Brussels (33mins) was on March 26th, 1966. It normally carried 101 passengers and had a fairly high cruising speed at Mach .88. This plane ceased flying in the mid-1970s.

Photo below is G-ARPA the first in the fleet taxiing in at LHR after landing in August 1967. It's worth noting that until 1966 the name "Trident" did not appear on the number 2 engine intake above the rear of the aircraft. After Trident 2's were introduced in 1967 all marks of the aircraft then had the name shown.

Of the Tridents built, 39 were Trident 1's, 24 going to BEA as 1C's the remainder to other operators as 1E's with increased seating and uprated engines.

Blind landings were achieved for the first-time using Tridents in 1965. Range of the 1C with max payload was 930 miles.

See later in the book for separate write ups on a Trident 2 flight and a Trident 3. In all I flew on 15 Tridents spread over the 3 types.

All Tridents had retired from operations by 1995.

There at five complete Tridents in Museums four of them in UK and one in China.

Hawker Siddeley Trident 1C March 1966. Taken of G-ARPA taxiing at LHR In August 1967.

Canadair CL44J

This aircraft was developed from the UK's Bristol Britannia using its wings and tail together with a new fuselage and engines. Initially, it first flew as a shorter CL44D on November 16th, 1959 and was bought up by freight operators and it had the feature of a swing tail, the hinges of which can be seen in the photo. However, Loftleider the Icelandic Airline wanted an economic airliner to do trans-Atlantic and ask for a stretched version just over 15ft longer which was called the 44J.

These aircraft were arriving with Loftleider in mid-1960s and TF-LLI the aircraft I flew on was delivered on March 13th, 1966, and I flew on it just two weeks later on March 26th out of Luxembourg via Keflavik to Kennedy New York.

This plane after service with Loftleider later went onto mainly freight operators until 1986. In all 39 CL44's had been built and they were powered by a more powerful Tyne at 5700shp compared with that in the Vanguard mentioned earlier.

Unless we look at the Russian turboprop the TU114 which wasn't operating generally in the western world, in 1966 the CL44J was the largest carrying aircraft at 189 passengers. It wasn't until the stretched DC8-61 came along in 1967 that it's place at the top had been taken.

Canadair CL44J March 1966. On arrival JFK.

May Flight Planning

On return from the USA and finding out I had passed the Operations Course in March, I was moved to the Flight Planning Department in an adjacent area of the Queens building.

This was where the BEA flight crews report for their flights and we had a counter facing into that area. My job title was Flight Planning Officer. The job entitled working with the latest wind charts for various flight levels and terminal area forecasts and for each aircraft type, determining how much fuel would be burnt on the journey from A to B (termed burn off).

Then in BEA, we allowed 45mins of holding fuel plus fuel to divert to an alternate airport, forecast to have good weather at the likely time of arrival. Added to this would be a small allowance for taxi out fuel. There is a whole heap more which this book cannot go into but I can mention that take-off weight is governed not only by the runway you are taking off from but if it is a short sector for instance, you'll more than likely be limited by the permitted landing weight of the aircraft at its nearby destination.

The term for this is RTOW (regulated take-off weight). This is why if you see a really long-haul aircraft such as an A380 or very rarely now a 747, but many other long-haul types such as A350's and 787's, but if it was flying LHR to Paris. For example, it would be taking off in a very short distance and very eager to lift into the air, and probably climbing like an express lift because it's limited to its landing weight at Paris not it's maximum permitted take-off weight.

So, we officers prepared the flight plans and for BEA, they would be for instance LHR to Paris, Copenhagen, Zurich, Rome, Glasgow, and many more, and present them to the operating crews in the reporting area and advise them the fuel at this stage to be loaded. If the crew were unhappy with that amount of fuel due to considerations re weather or ATC (air traffic control) or other reasons we would determine if higher fuel load is possible.

In any event fuel, generally out of UK was lower in cost than many places in Europe, so extra would be carried to minimise the uplift from the destination port always of course observing the RTOW requirements outlined above. It was interesting work and no two days were ever the same! That's a basic outline of what I did at BEA for the next eight years until 1974.

1967

September to Milan

FLIGHT PLANNING FAMILIARISATION (Famil) TRIP

From time-to-time, flight plan officers were designated to fly with the crew on the flight deck to experience the full operation, and I think in all instances with BEA it involved an out and back return journey. I can't recall any at that time when a night stop was used. My first famil was the Argosy freighter, a fairly useful aircraft but rather slow compared with say the Viscount that had the same four Rolls Royce Darts powering it!

They likened the Argosy's bulbous nose at the front to pushing a barn door through the air! With the noise of the Darts the Argosy was soon dubbed "The Whistling Wheelbarrow!" The route to Milan was somewhat difficult more so on the return as being lighter in weight at the end of its outward journey from London due fuel burnt off, it could go over the Alps and descend into Milan.

On the return taking off at max take-off weight which it often was, it couldn't come straight over the Alps so usually had to track west then north over France avoiding most of the high terrain. What I do remember, especially of the night time journey home is heading west out of Milan at 13000ft flying between fluffy piled up Cumulus clouds all backlit by a full moon behind us!

Then on arriving over northern France still at our cruising altitude which was by then 16000ft the night was breath takingly clear! It was just magnificent you could see every street and house light ahead of us in southern UK from Margate in East Kent right over west to the lights on the Isle of Wight. It was like looking at a map in an atlas! Flight time out 3hrs 35mins and back was 4hrs 2mins.

See details of the Argosy aircraft below.

Armstrong Whitworth Argosy AW650-222

This aircraft originally started as a 100 series and first flew on January 8th, 1959. BEA took delivery of three of the 100 series but they were wanting delivery of the 200 series which could accommodate International standard pallets.

G-ATTC a 200 series was delivered to BEA on November 21st, 1966 and my flight Heathrow to Milan Linate was on September 19th, 1967. After flying until the early 1970s, the Vanguard turned Merchantman, took over the freight operations and this Argosy went to other operators until flying in NZ and Australia stopped in November 1990. Photo below of a sister ship G-ASXM courtesy of Fred Barnes.

The Argosy was another aircraft that used Rolls Royce Darts for its power. In all 78 units were built but only 17 were built for civil use the majority of the rest were used by the Royal Air force which used them until 1978.

There are four museum exhibits to be seen in the UK and one in South Island NZ.

I visited the NZ aircraft and have since provided the museum there with copies of the flight plan from the above famil which are on display.

Armstrong Whitworth Argosy Aw650-222 September 1967. Shown is G-ASXM courtesy of Fred Barnes.

1968

February to New Zealand

During the mid-1960s, BEA and BOAC decided to have a Joint Medical Unit. I guess they thought the bodies were quite similar so this seemed a logical move! Shortly after a decision was made that once you had served five years with one airline, you could take one trip per year with the other airline as well.

Say no more! Five years to the day after I had joined BEA, I was on board a BOAC plane headed to NZ to see my bro!

G-ARWE was on flight BA944, its first leg LHR to Zurich on a journey out to Sydney and after a stop there, a further flight onto Auckland to visit my brother and family. Please note that the flight routing of my flight was London-Zurich-Beirut-Delhi-Rangoon-Hong Kong-Darwin-Sydney and believe it or not this is called a DIRECT flight, yes that's right DIRECT! (See glossary/general information for explanation).

The photo I used for my first 707 flight in 1962 was taken on the apron at Rangoon on this Journey. This was at the height of the Vietnam war. After take-off from Rangoon, we had to track SE until we reached the 13 parallel north of equator then head east over Vietnam until we reached international waters then head NE to Hong Kong. On arrival Sydney, I enjoyed four nights staying with my second cousin, Joyce, and her husband, Bill, who I would see much more of in the coming years.

After that, I travelled on to Auckland on a normal BA 707-436 and then following day, flew Auckland-Gisborne-Napier on an F27 my next new type details below to meet up with my brother Stewart and his family.

Overall, I stayed four weeks with them which included a week up at Lake Rotorua in lakeside accommodation. On reflection (pardon the pun), I'm going to include a Lake Rotorua sunset below! I also took a few days out to fly down to Wellington to have an interview with NAC (New Zealand National Airways corporation) the domestic airline, then flew up to Auckland on a Viscount which had come from LOT the Polish Airline, and had an interview with Air New Zealand before returning to Napier, and Stewart and his family.

He was working for NZ Aerial Mapping and the director had met me at Stewart's home and offered me a ride in their Beechcraft mapping aircraft down to the South Island. However, this trip didn't materialise, which explains a short while later I found myself in Norway in June to see some fjords up there!

Sunset on Lake Rotorua New Zealand February 1968.

After leaving Napier on March 16th, again on an F27 via Gisborne to Auckland and a BOAC 707 this time to Nandi where I had a full day. I met up with two staff from Air Canada from Toronto and hired a Mini Moke and had a great time driving up the west coast north from Nandi.

Early hours of next morning, BOAC 707 RWD (sister ship to RWE) flies me Nandi-Honolulu-San Francisco-JFK. I had the day in New York so met up with Alice, then had my first ride on a Super VC10 overnight to London (see details of that aircraft below). 20 Sectors on a Round World Journey!

Fokker Friendship F27

This was the most popular DC3 replacement aircraft by far and sold worldwide.

It first flew November 19th, 1959 and 586 were built in Europe and 207 were built in USA by Fairchild Hiller as the FH227 under a license agreement. Again, another plane that successfully used the very reliable Rolls Royce Dart turboprop engine for its power units.

ZK-BXD, the plane I flew on was owned by NAC. It was delivered to them on March 14th, 1961 and my flight was Auckland-Gisborne-Napier on February 18th, 1968. This was a series 100 aircraft that carried 44 passengers.

Later versions were developed that were stretched and carried higher numbers. NAC retired this plane in April 1980. Photo shows BXD on arrival at Napier airport.

In 2018, only ten F27's were still in operation worldwide, however, in 1987, a newer version named the Fokker F50 came onto the market which has again proved to be a great success (see my Bergen-Aberdeen sector August 1999). In all I flew on 16 sectors on F27's and they were all on NAC aircraft in New Zealand.

There are F27's in museums in at least nine countries around the world for visitors to see.

Fokker Friendship F27 February 1968. On arrival Napier NZ.

Vickers Armstrong Super VC10

This was more a competitor to the Boeing 707 than the earlier Comet 4C but even the Super version had better runway performance than the 707 due to the clean wing with the engines all tail mounted. The Standard model was even better suited to BOAC's Africa routes with the need for excellent runway performance at hot high airports. Whether flying on a Super or the Standard the load factors were always higher than competitors 707's as passengers enjoyed the quiet cabin with the Rolls Royce jets down at the back of the aircraft.

The type first flew on June 29th, 1962 and the first flight of G-ASGG was on May 17th, 1965, and I flew JFK to Heathrow on March 19th, 1968.

This aircraft was then later transferred to the RAF (Royal Air force) and scrapped April 1981. Photo below shows sister ship SGF taking off from Heathrow on a clear winter's day.

In all only 54 VC10's were built and of these 12 were Standard ones for BOAC and 17 were Super models. I had 12 further flights in Supers but see August 1974 for my ride in a Standard model. The Super could carry up to a maximum of 163 passengers but typically it would be lower in a two-class layout.

Of the 54 built, some units were built for the RAF but later many more were taken up by them when disposed of by civil airlines and used in roles of transport and inflight refuelling and the last was retired from flying as recently as 2013.

There are many complete exhibits in UK to see plus one in Germany.

Vickers Armstrong Super VC10 March 1968. Shown is take off of G-ASGF on a clear winter's day at LHR.

Sad Sequel to G-ARWE

Although, some of these details I haven't been able to confirm from BA, as far as I'm aware, after return of this aircraft from its February trip to Sydney, it went into the BOAC maintenance hangers at LHR for a major overhaul after which it did one air test flight which is the normal procedure. Thereafter, on April 12th, it took off on BA712 on its way to Sydney with first stop scheduled at Zurich and immediately after take-off from Heathrow the number two engine on the inner left wing dropped from the wing and fell into water close to Staines to the SW of the airport.

Capt. Taylor and his crew commenced a left-hand turn and came back down onto runway 05R (05Right see glossary) and brought the aircraft to a halt with flames coming from the left-hand wing.

Nearly everyone evacuated from the plane except four passengers were onboard including a handicapped person and Stewardess Barbara Jane Harrison was seen at the door but then turned back into the aircraft but perished together with the other four. She was posthumously awarded the George Cross for her valour.

In the flight crews' favour, they were handling a reasonably manoeuvrable plane as it would have been close to its landing weight, being it was only on a short sector to Zurich. Of the 127 on board, 122 survived which seems incredible when you see the flames involved in the incident. The flight had been in the air for just three minutes.

One of the other crew members was Acting first officer John Hutchinson who went on to become a Concorde Captain. Capt. Cliff Taylor had been in command on the same aircraft on my trip in February from Delhi via Rangoon to Hong Kong.

April, Stockholm Famil:

This time I travelled on my second famil on a Trident 1C G-ARPM with Capt. Turnbull plus his first and second officer. Stockholm is 866 miles distant from London, so is just comfortably inside maximum range of Trident 1's with full payload. The date of the trip was June 24th and flight time out to Arlanda Stockholm was 1hr 50mins, and return flight time was 2hrs 10mins.

This generally reflects the westerly winds that usually prevail, which create that difference at most times of the year. However, I might take this opportunity to explain something about flight schedules which is sometimes not understood.

The scheduled times are when the aircraft pushes back from the gate or comes back onto the gate at its destination (STD and STA: Scheduled Time of Arrival). Built into schedules airlines produce, are allowance for taxy times. Heathrow is usually busy whereas Stockholm not quite as much.

So, on the day of our flight, we had an allowance of 25mins on the outward journey for taxy times but only 10mins on the return journey as the airline publish virtually the same scheduled time for each direction. It's not just what happens in the air but how much time is spent taxiing on the ground!

On one of the DC9 flights below taking off from LHR to Stavanger, we were just lining up onto RW 28L (Runway 28Left see glossary) some 20mins after STD, and passenger next to me was bitterly complaining that we were late and I had to assure him we were perfectly on time! We had left the gate on schedule and 20mins at LHR for taxy time was not overly long.

June 1968 to January 1969 to Norway

Having failed to get the flight down to the South Island of NZ in March in the aero survey aircraft, I decided to visit Norway and see some Fjords there! First off, I headed up there on June 18th in the DC9 shown below from Heathrow via Stavanger to Bergen for a twelve-night stay. I managed to find an apartment overlooking Bergen harbour which I was to share with my pal, Hedley, who also worked for BEA who arrived a couple of days later.

We did a Fjord cruise and the 30mins flight in the Cessna 185 floatplane photo also shown below. One night, we were out at a nightspot and I met a local girl called Ingar and we seemed to hit it off, so kept in touch during our stay.

Hedley and I returned to LHR on a SAS DC9 via Stavanger on June 30th.

Douglas DC9-40

Douglas originally first flew a series 10 of the DC9 on February 25th, 1965 which carried 90 passengers but they quickly developed stretched versions so the series 40 could carry 125.

SE-DBW first flew on May 2nd, 1968 and my flight LHR-Stavanger-Bergen was on June 18th, 1968. Note that whilst this is a Swedish registered aircraft in the tradition of SAS it is operating a service from UK to Norway. This plane after service with SAS was retired by Northwest Airlines in February 1991.

I flew 19 sectors on DC9's all within six return trips to Norway from UK. Although it had a two year start on the 737 which didn't fly until 1967, it achieved a reasonable number of sales at 976. Also, the MD 80 went on later to supersede it but clearly Boeings 737 with nearly 11000 sold has come out a clear winner and is continuing to sell.

Museum exhibits of the DC9 are available to see in Canada, Spain, Italy. US, Indonesia and Mexico.

Douglas DC9-40 June 1968. On arrival Bergen after summer storm.

Cessna 185 Skywagon

The aircraft I flew on was in a floatplane configuration but most would have been operating as landplanes, but a lot of lakes and coastlines such as Alaska and Norway made floatplanes almost an essential mode of transport. This type first flew in July 1960 and was a six-seater and production finished in 1985 after 4400 units had been manufactured.

LN-TSM was delivered in 1961 and my flight was a scenic one out of Bergen harbour on June 28th, 1968 for 31mins. It has been operated by various

Norwegian operators since then until May 2016. Photo below show the aircraft at rest in Bergen harbour with yours truly.

Cessna 185 Skywagon June 1968. Taken in Bergen harbour.

August to Bergen

ROMANCE NUMBER TWO!

In August, I made what was to be the first of five further trips to Bergen to visit Ingar which continued through until January 1969. Most were DC9's via Stavanger in the summer and I did one Bergen to LHR non-stop on the same

Stockholm Famil Trident G-ARPM, but come the winter routings, I had to travel via Oslo.

Not all were DC9's. On one trip, I got Comet 4B's non-stop London-Oslo-London, and within Norway Three SAS Caravelles were travelled on and with the Bergen-Oslo route, I flew three Convair CV440's the first as per the details below. Ingar also came over to the UK to visit me in September, for about a week. Came via a Bergen-Newcastle ferry but went back on SAS DC9. After the January 1969 trip, I wrote but did not hear back.

Convair CV440 Metropolitan

This type initially started off in the late 1940s as the 240 model and first flew in 1947.

Overall including all the later versions, it was probably the best initial attempt at a DC3 replacement with a total of 1181 models built. The 240 carried 40 passengers then the 340 and 440 shared the same stretched fuselage where capacity had been increased to 52.

The 440 first flew October 6th, 1955 and SE-BSO was delivered to SAS on July 26th, 1956.

My flight from Oslo (the old Fornebu Airport in Oslo Fjord) to Bergen was on October 25th, 1968.

It carried on with SAS and various other operators and went into storage in the Dominican Republic in May 1992, I flew on two more SAS CV440's on the Oslo-Bergen route in the course of the Norway trips in 1968/January 1969.

Photo shows Norwegian registered sister ship, LN-KLA, courtesy of Fred Barnes which I did fly on back to Oslo on this particular October trip.

162 of the total aircraft built were CV440's but many of the earlier 340's were upgraded to 440 standard. Many since have been re-engined to Turboprop power mainly with Allison engines and these are designated from CV540 and above.

There are aircraft of this basic type in numerous museums displayed in many countries throughout the world.

Convair CV440 Metropolitan October 1968. LN-KLA was my second flight on the type four days later on return to Oslo.
Photo courtesy of Fred Barnes.

1969

January to South America

I had the chance of a ticket to South America with Varig the Brazilian airline and on January 14th, I headed out of LHR on an Iberia Airlines Caravelle to Madrid. Early hours of next morning, on a Varig 707 I took off to Rio. Madrid had at the time one of the longest runways around and depending on temperature, weight of aircraft, and other factors, airlines can determine a percentage of thrust to safely take off.

It doesn't have to be full thrust at every take off which will quickly degrade engine life. I have a habit of timing take off roll times (something to pass the time I guess) and this take off roll took 63 seconds and used probably 95% of the runway length before we lifted into the air! After 10hrs 4mins we were in Rio.

I stayed in Rio for five nights and went to the top of Sugar Loaf Mountain and also Corcovado with its Statue of Christ the redeemer at the top. Also saw all the famous beaches too! Early one morning I took a taxi ride up Corcovado and you'll see below an image of a dawn shot of the Sugar loaf mountain from there.

A predawn view of Sugarloaf Mountain Rio de Janeiro January 1969.

Now I headed off to Santiago in Chile which brought me to flying on my next type a Douglas DC8 again with Varig, this time stopping at Buenos Aires enroute. Overall, I had five nights in Chile with the first two spent in Santiago seeing the sights. What is spectacular is that the snow-capped peaks are seemingly so close to the city.

A word of advice about drinking Pisco Sour the national drink in Chile. Always try and find a bar on the same side of the street as your hotel. I had two drinks and seriously cannot remember crossing the road back to my hotel or anything else until the next morning!

On the Saturday morning, Sheila who I had met on the trip to Paris in June 1965 picked me up at my hotel and drove me in her 2CV out to the west coast to Valparaiso, and then just a little north to ConCon where her parents lived and we stayed there over the Saturday night. On the Sunday, we returned to Santiago and after two more nights, I flew back via Buenos Aires to Rio on the same DC8 PDS to connect with a Varig 707 this time to Lisbon.

Wait it's not over yet! This bit's weird. Early next morning, we are nearly 8 hrs into our 9hrs 25mins sector to Lisbon, and I have a right-hand window seat and the sun has just risen. I head to the toilet and return to my seat some minutes later. Where has the Sun gone? It's on the other side of the airplane!

We had passed the Canary Islands enroute and were part of the way towards Lisbon when captain decided the weather was too turbulent in Lisbon for a landing, so turned around in the air and we diverted back to Las Palmas in the Canaries. I'd been sitting in Las Palmas and got talking to a female First officer flying for Skyways in the UK on Avro 748's (see Jun 2005). We finally left and arrived Lisbon 1hr 53mins later, not without seeing the wings bend up and down quite a bit on the descent.

Next, we had to fly onto Paris (Orly) a flight time of 1hr 57mins arriving there around 5hrs behind STA. I then managed a seat on the last Air France Boeing 727-200 (a new type for me so see details below) to LHR and then the last bus home! Quite a trip!

A 707 FOOTNOTE

In the light of the mid-air turnaround that happened on the above travel from Rio to Lisbon, I thought it might be of interest to readers to find out what happens when they do occur which isn't that frequent as the information below will also show.

I asked a friend of mine a retired 747 Captain what the procedure was to do a 180 degree turn whilst cruising at 30000ft and he said, "I don't know I've never done one!" but later he did send me the information on such a manoeuvre. Essentially, they cannot turn on a dime!

A not too steep bank angle has to be selected and the process set in motion, and the plane will not be facing in the opposite direction until at least 4mins later, and it will be around 20 nmi away on the other side of an imaginary half circle before the plane is facing back towards its point of origin.

Douglas DC8-33

This aircraft was another early contender to the long-haul jet market. The first plane took to the air on May 30th, 1958 around six months after the Boeing 707. It didn't sell as well with a total of 556 being built but later models were considerably stretched compared to the series 33 photo shown. It entered service with Delta and United on September 18th, 1959. Some of the 60-series carried well over 200 passengers started flying in the late 1960s.

PP-PDS was delivered in July 1965 and my first flight of four sectors on this plane was on January 23rd, 1969 between Rio and Buenos Aires enroute to Santiago. Varig carried 149 passengers on their DC8's. After thirteen years with them, this aircraft went to various operators and was scrapped in February 1992.

Photo below shows the take-off from Santiago on January 23rd, on its return via Buenos Aires to Rio.

In all ten sectors have been flown on DC8s, these four with Varig, four with SAS and two with Air NZ.

There are DC8 exhibits in seven museums in the countries of Japan, China, France, US, and Zambia.

Douglas DC8-33 January 1969. On its return take off back to Rio from Santiago.

Boeing 727-200

This aircraft designed by Boeing as a short to medium haul airliner had a three-engine layout laid out at the rear of the plane with the centre engine featuring an S shaped air intake.

The first 100 series aircraft had its maiden flight on February 9th, 1963 and entered service with Eastern Airlines on February 1st, 1964, and it typically carried 106 passengers. The stretched 200 series followed and flew on July 27th, 1967 and typical passenger load was 134 in two classes.

F-BOJA first flew on March 9th, 1968 then delivered to Air France. My flight was from Orly Paris to LHR on January 29th, 1969 with flight time of 42mins. It was retired from service in 1991.

I flew three other sectors on this type one was on United and two were in Australia.

Photo below is of sister ship 'OJD' courtesy of John Roach shown taxiing at LHR.

By comparison with the low number of Tridents built, by starting with a much smaller machine and building up to the Trident 3B, Boeing had started with a basic larger aircraft which they marketed well and an impressive 1832 units were sold worldwide.

There are museum exhibits of this 727 type mainly in the US but also to be found in Denmark, UK and Mexico.

Boeing 727-200 January 1969. Photo courtesy of John Roach shows a sister ship taxiing at LHR.

February to Innsbruck

The flights below are a return from LHR to Munich (Riem airport closed 1992) on my next new type a BAC 111-500 series. There I caught a train from Munich for the short journey south under the Alps to Innsbruck in Austria, which was my destination for a three-night stay. On our 1965 trip with David, I had called into the BEA town office there and had become friends with one of girls there called Heidi (what else!).

So, she and some other friends showed me around and on one full day, I did a day trip south into Italy to Cortina in the Dolomites. I mentioned in the 1965 trip the village of Igls outside of Innsbruck, and on our way back we came through this village and in its winter scenery with horse drawn sleighs going through the streets it just looked like a fairy tale setting!

BAC111-500

BAC (British Aircraft Corporation) first flew a series 200 version of this short to medium haul airliner on August 20th, 1963. It was introduced into service by British United Airways carrying 80 passengers on January 22nd, 1965, and was competing with other types such as the DC9, Caravelle, Trident etc. Later, a stretched series called the 500 was introduced in 1967 with passenger load substantially increased to 119 seats.

G-AVMM was delivered to BEA on October 25th, 1968 and I flew Heathrow to Munich on February 3rd, 1969. I returned a few days later on G-AVMS, a sister ship. These aircraft were not in the normal BEA colour scheme.

They had a dark blue tail to reflect they also were used to operate services into Berlin on behalf of Air France. VMM went onto European Air charter then stored in March 2008. Photo below is VMS taxiing in at Munich on arrival from Heathrow, the plane for my return journey.

244 of this type were produced in the UK with an additional nine licence built in Romania.

The last aircraft retired from flying in 2019.

There are complete museum exhibits in UK, Chile, Denmark and Romania.

In the late 1970s in my Panam Auckland days I was to see more of BAC111's as we provided Ramp handling for the Air Pacific services operating from Fiji and Tonga.

BAC111-500 February 1969. G-AVMS taxiing at Munich was the plane for return sector to LHR. Apologies for quality. It was a very dull day!

April to Greenland

In a sense this was a BEA sponsored Famil as with my interest in Arctic regions I asked if they could approach SAS to see if I could visit Sondre Stromfjord (now Kangerlussauq). It's located at the head of a long Fjord on Greenland's west coast and just inside the Arctic circle.

I left LHR on a SAS DC9 to Copenhagen and stayed overnight close to the airport. Next morning, after meeting with the crew in the briefing area the DC8 a Swedish registered one departed and scheduled route that day was via Keflavik in Iceland.

After a 1hr 42mins flight from there we came up the Fjord to touch down on the Sondrestrom runway (approach view below).The initial part of the runway which existed in WW2 is uphill and difficult to judge a landing on. The second half to make it an adequate runway for today's planes was added later and the civil terminal is towards the end on the left and the USAF (United States Air Force) area is over on the right.

Royal Greenland Trade Department looked after me with meals and accommodation. There is the hotel there for passengers who cannot connect out to the west coast on the same day or if weather delays occur. Both SAS and the USAF showed me round and Greenlandair took me out to DYE 1 (Dewline station see glossary) on an S61N helicopter on a supply charter flight described below. Yet another type to my tally!

In addition to the S61N photo you will see a view taken from DYE 1 of the west Greenland coast. A more remote and beautiful spot you could not imagine!

After three nights at Sondrestrom, it was time to fly back to Copenhagen and again the routing was back via Keflavik. Each SAS DC8 flies a triangle route, but it happened I had picked a day each time when it flew via Iceland, when the other direction had been non-stop Copenhagen-Sondrestrom or vv. Later on, you'll see a far more bizarre thing that happened on a Panam 747SP.

Anyway, back to the present on the last sector Keflavik-Copenhagen, I started to feel peckish and you know how aircraft galleys are always full of some sort of snacks! Well, there was nothing!

The SAS hostie opened every drawer. We had to stay hungry till we landed. The only food on board was fuel in the tanks! After a night near the airport, I flew on a SAS DC9 back to LHR next morning. A magnificent trip, one I still have fond memories of!

Short finals approach Sondrestrom Air Base West Greenland April 1969.

View from DYE 1's Helipad 5000ft up on Greenland's west Coast. April 1969.

Sikorksky S61N

This helicopter was developed from the military Sea King helicopter which first flew on March 11th, 1959 and many were used in oil rig work and other industrial applications. The S61N first flew on August 7th, 1962 and in all 119 of this aircraft were built. The civil aircraft carried around 24 passengers.

OY-HAF was purchased from the US in 1965 and my flight from Sondrestrom Air base in western Greenland was a return to an early warning Dew line station DYE1 5000ft up on the west coast of Greenland on April 16th, 1969. Flight time was 31mins each way and was a supply flight for the USAF operated by Greenlandair.

Photo is HAF on the Heli pad at Dye 1 showing a view from the edge of the pad looking SW to the west Greenland coast and the Davis Strait extreme right.

In the 1960s, most towns on the west Greenland coast only had a helicopter landing pad, and on the days when airline flights arrived into Sondrestrom from Copenhagen, numerous shuttles would be operated by Greenlandair using up to nine S61N's to move passengers in and out of Sondrestrom on the day of the flight.

More recently, most towns now have 800 metre runways and are served by Dash 8 turboprops so HAF and one other sister ship are the only remaining S61N's. They also assist in search and rescue when required.

Sikorksky S61N April 1969. On the helipad at DYE1 on West Greenland coast.

May to New Zealand

On this trip, I took my mum with me on her first flight (clutching onto me as we took off!)

We headed out of LHR to JFK in one of BOAC's normal 707-436 models G-APFO and arrived JFK after a flight of 7hrs 27mins. Here we picked up my father who had travelled out late April and had stayed with Alice his cousin. We travelled on to LA together which strangely enough was my 100th flight! Rather apt that I had both parents travelling with me as well!

All this was on PFO right on through Honolulu to Nandi. We stayed one day in Nandi then travelled down on G-APFH to Auckland (see photo), and continued on same day on a Fokker Friendship to Napier my brothers home port. My folks stayed on in NZ longer but I needed to come home so left Auckland to Sydney May 27th on another normal BA 707 PFJ.

In fact, I enjoyed a 26-hour birthday because of the time difference, and had two nights with Bill and Joyce, then boarded RWD (again) up through Nandi and Honolulu to San Francisco. But going back to the take-off from Sydney it was in the middle of a tremendous storm. The sound of the rain on the roof of the plane as we boarded was quite deafening!

After take-off, which was RW34 (towards the city which is unusual in itself), we climbed out through lower cloud then came out into full moonlight between towering cumulonimbus clouds that went way up into the night sky. It was an amazing sight to see. On arrival San Francisco, Alice's friend Chloe showed me round for a day.

Then the friends I'd made in United in Chicago arranged a ticket for me to travel to Chicago and the plane was a Boeing 720 details as below, so I spent two nights there catching up with them. Also, on this stay met up with Sally junior from the UK family, back in the 1940s when we had travelled down in convoy to the South Coast, they in their tiny Austin 'Box saloon' and our family in our slightly larger Standard.

Sally was now working as a missionary in Ecuador but on leave staying with a family in Chicago. It was good to meet up again. I then travelled to Newark on a United Boeing 727-200 and spent three nights in New York visiting my second cousins. I think I had planned to leave JFK on the morning flight to Heathrow which left at 10 AM but it was delayed with a technical problem, so it was a question of waiting for a choice of the evening flights all of which were quite full.

Everyone wanted non-stop to Heathrow and were not making a decision. I was asked if I would take a flight via Manchester and gladly took it so I rode on super VC10 G-ASGK. Respective flight times 5hrs 49mins across to Manchester and then 46 mins onto LHR.

My Parents arrive in Auckland for first time. May 1969.

Boeing 720

This type was derived from the 707 which had flown in December 1957. The 720 is a lighter, shorter aircraft designed for better short field performance and first flew on November 23rd, 1959. It entered service with United on July 5th, 1960 and typical load was 131 passengers in two classes and 154 of this type were built.

N7223U was delivered in 1962 and my flight from San Francisco to Chicago O'Hare was on May 30th, 1969. This aircraft after seven more years of United service was transferred to Belize Airways and is still flying in early 2021! Photo below courtesy of Boeing Company and Stewart Wilson.

I did two further flights on 720's on Olympic airways from Athens return to Heraklion on the island of Crete in 1972.

Museums with 720's in the world are Taiwan, Pakistan, Canada and Colombia.

Boeing B720 May 1969. Photo courtesy of Boeing and Stewart Wilson.

Taking Stock

Now we stay at home for a while. Look at the flying I've done! In the last sixteen months, I've totalled up 194 flying hours which works out at least the equivalent of four round world trips.

To be honest, I'm a bit happier with my feet on the ground but working for an airline had given me the opportunity to travel so I was really foolish not to take advantage of it.

Famous comedian, Mel Brooks, said once, "If God had meant us to fly, He'd have given us tickets!" Later on, I became more comfortable about being aloft. Well at that time, I was 27 years of age and basically comfortable at home but I should be in my own place. My parent's place is 12 miles from the airport which from time to time I've travelled by bus, fortunately one bus all the way to the centre of the airport, also other times by car and for a number of years by 250cc motorbike!

Well, those are my thoughts as we progress through the rest of the year, but then we come to the usual LHR around November, with some fog in its weather which changed my life.

Obviously, in Flight Planning department if there are no flight plans to prepare because there are no planes flying, they put the staff to good use elsewhere, so they send us through a few doors into another area of flight ops which is flight enquiries. They get inundated with calls right now so need all the help they can get!

By now, we are nearly into the 1970s and the old Ops "Atrium" has gone and it's all on one level with flight enquiries behind a glass screen at one end with a long-curved china-graph board where the departure and arrival details were put up with marker pen i.e., +5 etc.

To do this, they had a bank of people (of which I became one) answering phones facing the board and two people walking backwards and forwards along this board adding information (we do get to the digital age eventually). Well, I asked the shift supervisor sitting next to me, who was the rather nice-looking young lady with the marker pen in her hand?

The reply was it was Anne and she had joined in Sep so it was a bit of a surprise I had not seen her in the intervening months. Well later we bumped into each other literally on the start of a night shift, on the very occasion I was planning to ask if we could get a tea break at the same time. As they say, the rest is history! But we have been happily married for forty-nine years now, and the first sight was it all began "On a foggy day in London Town!"

1970

Romance Number Three

Early this year was a defining point in my life as I started to go out with Anne and the thoughts, I'd had the previous year about having my own place were put into action. I even considered buying a houseboat and looked at a few as the Thames river meandered around fairly close to the west and south of LHR, but in the end, my conservative side decided bricks and mortar was a better way to go.

I had an insurance policy which could be borrowed on, so with that, and money saved, I was able to purchase a fairly modern terraced town house around two miles north of LHR at a town called West Drayton which also serves as the home of the ATC (Air Traffic Control) centre for southern England's upper airspace. This was a great location as it was out of the noise path of the east west runways at the airport.

It was a very comfortable centrally heated house and one of the last houses on the western edge of the county of Middlesex with a view of open country from the back windows with a stream at the bottom of the garden. So, I moved in May 1970 and even knew a neighbour next door but one, as someone from the church we had all attended in earlier years. I settled in to my new surroundings and made a few minor changes to start with, then thought about maybe travelling again!

July to Athens

Together with a few friends (one was from BOAC), we headed down to Athens and the Trident 2 was a new type for me so details are found below. We had four nights down there and I'm not sure if they had all done this trip before, but I guess I just went along with what the group wanted to do. Well, I look back on that trip now with regret.

The airport then was located about 10 kms SE of Athens at a suburb on the coast called Glyfada. Basically, now when I look at a map the runway was parallel to the coast about 600 m inland and we were staying at a hotel nearer the beach and spent the days on the beach. The Acropolis was only 10 kms away and not one person suggested going to see it! That's one big regret of my travels. In 1972, Anne and I went to Crete and transited Athens both ways, but that didn't allow us time to visit either.

Hawker Siddeley Trident 2E

This stretched version of the Trident 1 described earlier first flew on July 27th, 1967. It could carry up to 115 Passengers with maximum payload on a range of 2430 miles so became a substantial contribution to BEA's fleet. Of the 117 Tridents built 50 were model 2's quite a number of those going to China.

G-AVFE was delivered to BEA May 8th, 1968 and my flight London to Athens was on July 29th, 1970. This continued to operate with the BEA/BA family until going into storage at Belfast Airport in February 1985. In all I flew on eight Trident 2E sectors which were London-Athens route or down to Faro on Portugal's Algarve and one sector down to Gibraltar. See photo below of sister ship VFI.

There is only one Trident 2E on display which is at Duxford in UK, but a type 1 and 3's are also in UK plus a 1E in China.

Hawker Siddeley Trident 2E July 1970. Photo taken in 1968 at Farnborough of G-AVFI landing on a wet runway.

1971

January to New Zealand

I think this was planned to depart on the January 4th, but with fog at LHR, I returned to my house that night, but one of my neighbours saw me return and figured I'd closed my house up and made it safe from freezing up in the winter, which was the case so they kindly offered for me to stay with them until I could get away!

I went next day to the airport, still didn't meet with success so spent another night with them and finally got away on the third try on the January 6th. This was 17 sectors in all but with no new types. Firstly, a BOAC 707-436 LHR-Frankfurt-Tel Aviv-Tehran-Bombay-Hong Kong, then a Super VC10 via Darwin to Sydney.

After two nights with Bill and Joyce, another 707-436 to Auckland and after a night there Fokker Friendships to and from Napier, to spend time with Stewart, my brother, and his family. While I was there, I was conscious of the great climate NZ enjoyed and its effect on the longevity on motor cars and have always had an interest in an Austin seven. I always had a hankering for a 'Box Saloon' like the one we followed down to the South coast in the Post war years!

But there weren't that many around and had to be content with the newer larger version that I got (see photo at end of the 1973 pages) and I bought one complete with chooks in it, in a barn and shipped it home (minus the chooks)! More of this story in 1973.

Now on my way back try this for a milk run! Napier to Auckland is 204 miles. The routing of my flight on NAC's Fokker Friendship was via Gisborne and Whakatane. That's three sectors instead of one! I was almost exhausted before I'd left New Zealand!

So, same evening left on a 707-436 up to Nandi and stayed one night, and then a Super VC10 through Honolulu-Los Angeles-JFK-to LHR. Arriving late PM on February 16th, having flown on the daylight flight from JFK with a flight time of 5hrs 56mins which reflects flying with pretty good tailwinds for most of that sector.

If you really wanted to get to London in a hurry, you should have taken the BA flight on February 10th, 2020 from JFK. On that Saturday night, with the help of a Jetstream thanks to Storm Ciara the Sub sonic record came under 5hrs and this 747-400 achieved a flight time JFK-LHR of 4hrs 56mins!

July to Faro Portugal

Well, after my return from NZ things are blossoming with my relationship with Anne.

As they say we are going steady! We decided to take a holiday together and fly down to Faro on Portugal's southern coast known as the Algarve. It's a lovely region with warm sun and beautiful beaches. We had ten nights down there, but on reflection our stay on the east end of the coast at a place called Quarteira was probably not the best spot to choose.

It was pleasant enough and we did some good touring around, but the best spots are really to the west of Faro airport which is centrally located along the south facing coast. We flew down on a normal BEA Trident 2 on July 20th but return again on July 30th on the same type but this time an aircraft belonging to Cyprus Airways with registration 5B-DAB.

BEA performed the maintenance for Cyprus airways so at certain times there had to be a bit of sharing of aircraft between the fleets. The same had applied with the Comet 4Bs of Olympic airways.

Proposal

Now I think we come to the kneeling on the ground moment! I proposed to Anne and asked her to marry me on her birthday on August 9th, 1971! Well, as you know from later, I did get a YES!

She had spent her earlier years with her mum and dad, and a younger brother, David, in Newport in Monmouthshire. Sadly, her father died of a cancer at an early age in 1958 when Anne had only just turned 15. In hindsight, in those days his death was probably attributable to working with chemicals without appropriate PPE (Personal Protective Equipment) which was not done at the time!

His death presented Anne's mother a challenge of bringing up Anne and her 11-year-old brother, and she decided on a fresh start and moved up to Pinner NW of London. Anne, when she finished school, worked in Banks then trained as a Pharmacist Dispenser but then got to hear of friends working for airlines so made the move to BEA (as mentioned earlier) in September 1969.

October to Paris

Later in the year, Anne and I had three nights in Paris, flying to and from Le Bourget airport in Trident 1's. Date over was October 8th, and returned on the 11th. We visited a young family over there who were friends of Anne's mother and they showed us around some of the more local sights such as flea markets in the NW suburban area of Paris where they lived. It was interesting to see a bit more of how the locals lived.

1972

April

Well, we come up to the BIG DAY!

My brother, Stewart, has arrived from NZ to be my best man. Anne and I are married at Pinner church NW of London on April 21st, 1972 and a small reception is held at an old property north of Harrow called 'Grimsdyke'. Built in the 1870s, this was the home of W.S. Gilbert of the Gilbert and Sullivan Operatic Duo.

He tragically died whilst trying to save a girl from drowning in the lake on the property. It fell into disuse in the 1960s but was renovated and reopened as a hotel in 1970. Gilbert and Sullivan evenings are held there from time to time and when we still lived in the UK, we attended one which was a great evening.

After the festivities of the wedding day, which went extremely well, Anne and I headed off to LHR and caught an evening flight to Faro. It was the very first Trident 2 BEA received G-AVFA. When we arrived Faro, I was in the arrivals hall at immigration and realised my brand-new wedding ring was still in the rear toilet of the plane!

I think the crew coming into the terminal were rather surprised to find me (who they knew of course) rushing back across the tarmac towards the plane, and lo and behold there was the ring still sitting there! Pretty bad show if I lost it on day one! This time we went west along the coast and stayed at Albufeira, a delightful place with some beautiful restaurants tucked through little alley ways looking south over the ocean where one can enjoy a leisurely lunch.

We had nine delightful nights down there and saw some of the coast further west. A really nice place to go! Time to head back to the UK, this time on a Trident 3, please see details below.

Before you read that though, now I'm a married man, I think you had better have a quote from Ron, my friend in BA. I've never done this myself but he introduces his wife as, "This is my first wife." Nice one, Ron!

Hawker Siddeley Trident 3B

The final development from the smaller Trident 1. The Trident 3B was still operating with three Rolls Royce Spey engines even though they were higher powered Spey512 than on earlier versions, they were not sufficient for the new size of this version so a booster engine was installed at the base of the fin to be used at take-off.

It could carry up to 180 passengers but typically 150 passengers was a more usual number in two classes. 28 Version 3's were built of the 117 total Tridents produced, and two of these were an extended range version.

G-AWZL had its first flight December 11th, 1969 and delivered to BEA early the next year. Our flight was a return leg from Faro on Portugal's Algarve to LHR on April 30th, 1972.

It continued flying with BEA and BA until October 1982. It became a useful addition to BEA's fleet and could operate to a range of nearly 1100 miles with maximum payload which suited many of their European routes.

Photo is of WZW taking off from Gibraltar in March 1973. This is the aircraft also featured on the cover of the book climbing above the Vanguards wing.

There are only two Trident 3B's in museums both in the UK but other Trident models as mentioned earlier, Type 1 and 2 are also in the UK and a type 1 in China are available to view.

With Anne moving in to the West Drayton house on our return from Portugal we started to adjust to married life together, so the feet stayed on the ground for a whole six months. We all worked different shifts in the Central area at LHR. It happened on a number of occasions I would be just going to work in the 'in' tunnel when I'd see Anne coming out to head home!

Ships passing in the night. However, there were better times of course, and on many occasions, we would have three days off at the same time and take a break away down on the south Coast. The Lulworth Cove photo was taken on such an occasion!

Hawker Siddeley Trident 3B. April 1972. Photo is G-AWZW taking off from Gibraltar in March 1973. This same plane is shown climbing away on front cover of book.

October to Crete

We head to Crete for a holiday. Crete is the largest of the Greek islands and around a 40-minute flight south of Athens and we head there for eleven nights. No new types on this trip. Trident 2's to and from Athens and then Olympic airways Boeing 720's from there to and from Heraklion the main airport in Crete.

Our date out was October 19th, and what amazed Anne about the Boeing was as Heraklion was only 192 miles from Athens, we would have been around landing weight on take-off from Athens (per my notes in Flight Planning 1966), hence being a long-haul aircraft and used to taking off at much heavier weights it went up like a rocket, surprising little Annie to no end!

We enjoyed our holiday in Crete, and experienced a Sirocco, a hot dry wind coming in from the south from North Africa. On April 30th, we had to return to London.

1973

March to Gibraltar

No new types but an interesting trip. We headed off on a Trident 2 from LHR and flight time to Gib as it's called was 2hrs 21mins. This is rated as one of the ten most dangerous airports in the world, mainly because of the huge rock right to the side of the runway which can create tremendous turbulence at times making it difficult for pilots to make an accurate approach.

We saw all the sights in Gib including cable car to the top of the rock and saw the Barbery apes. We made a day trip to Tangier in Morocco on the daily ferry but nearly came unstuck. Gibair use a leased Viscount from BEA and run a daily flight over and back in the evening which is what we were planning, to get us back to Gib.

What we didn't know was that Tangier local time was 30mins ahead of Gib, so we are still in a bus going out to Tangier airport when the arriving Viscount goes overhead. When we got to the airport, we had minutes to get on-board and we were on our way!

The cover of the book shows the left wing of the Vanguard G-APEH that we flew back to LHR on March 31st. It was an extra flight with only about 12 passengers on board. We sat at the back where it is quietest. On the cover the Trident 3 just airborne is the scheduled flight that day which doesn't have enough runway length to make London non-stop so makes a stop at Madrid.

Our flight time non-stop to LHR was 3hrs 40mins.

Moving from Heathrow?

Anne and I were having discussions about options regarding moving away from London. One was that North Sea Oil was booming and Aberdeen in

Scotland was becoming a very busy port for BEA, and I imagine if we had wanted to move up there, I could have found employment with them there. The other option was to emigrate to NZ and obtain airline work out there, so we put in place two trips.

Anne had never been to Scotland before so, although, we didn't visit the Aberdeen area, I thought we could show off some of its sights and let her experience some of what it looked like! So, first trip below is to Inverness.

July to Inverness

We headed up to Inverness on July 14th, 1973 on Viscount G-AOJB (affectionately we called this one JINGLE BELLS!), and flight time was 1hr 40mins. We travelled into the city and picked up a hire car from a local hire car firm for our one week stay. We then headed NW and got to Lochinver right out on the NW coast and had a three night stay there and one day visited the Summer Isles which you would imagine was somewhere in the Caribbean!

Also, walking down the street in Lochinver bumped into a BEA first officer. Terribly small world! After Lochinver, we travelled a long way south to a place called Kilchoan on the Ardnamurchan Peninsula, but in using the Isle of Skye for part of the journey, we had to use a ferry from Armadale to Mallaig to get back onto the mainland.

Missed one ferry and had to wait 3hrs for the next and ended up along a switchback road for seemingly miles at midnight to get there. However, Kilchoan was delightful and then we had one more night on way back to Inverness dropped off our car and got transport to the airport. Flight back on July 21st was another Viscount in 1hr 50mins.

October, a Visit for Anne to See NZ

We left on October 31st, and details of the new type for both of us, are detailed below. Certainly, on the via Asia routes see how the number of stops has been dramatically reduced. There are now only two from London to Sydney compared with six from two years previously!

This was at the peak of the Oil crisis with all the terminals we walked through on 50% lighting. We had planned to go straight through Sydney but this time at the start of a weekend all the flights were full trans-Tasman, so we stayed with Bill and Joyce for three nights and then went on the Monday on Air NZ DC8 to Wellington and an F27 up to Napier to my brother's place.

After just over three weeks with my brother, Anne and I headed to Auckland on an F27 on November 28th, and straight onto the Air NZ DC10 with details below. We had one day in Nandi and caught a Super VC10 early hours of the 30th via Honolulu-LA-JFK, and connected on to a 747-136 daylight flight to LHR arriving late on November 30th.

Boeing 747-136

An amazing part of Aviation history spanning fifty years. This venture was a very perilous one for Boeing and they were looking at uncharted territory for an airliner so large. It was dubbed the 'Jumbo'. Lockheed and Douglas went for slightly smaller options powered by three engines with one on each wing and one down at the tail.

These were all the first wide bodied jets to fly, featuring twin aisles. However, the 747 with its four wing mounted engines was first to fly on February 9th, 1969 and Panam operated the first service JFK to LHR on January 22nd, 1970. Since then, the 200 series still with the small upper deck bubble shape came next, followed then by the 300 and 400 both featuring stretched upper decks.

All these will be covered in more detail later. Other developments were the short fuselage long range version called the 747SP (Special Performance) which is outlined later in the book. More recently a new version using composite materials and called the 747-8 which is longer has been introduced but mainly by freight airlines although there are some passenger versions in service. A typical passenger load on the 100 and 200 series was around 350 in a three-class layout often using the upper deck for some form of passenger class.

In talking about passenger loads, Boeing did produce an SR version (short range) which was taken up by the Japanese domestic market which was tailored to all economy seating of up to 550 seats. Sadly, the onset of COVID-19 in 2020 caused most airlines to curtail their use of 747s earlier than they had planned but for fifty years they have been a very recognisable shape at our airports and in the skies and have been dubbed 'The Queen of The Skies'.

G-AWNM was delivered to BOAC in May 1973. Our flight LHR-Bahrain-Singapore-Sydney started on October 31st, 1973. It operated with BOAC then the BA family until it was flown to Cardiff December 1999 and now stored Roswell USA.

In all I flew on 25 sectors on this type some with BOAC then a higher number with Panam in the late 1970s and finally the last few with BA in the early 80s. Photo is of WNB on a take-off at LHR May 1972 returning my brother to NZ after his best man duties at our wedding.

There are many 747s on display at various museums especially in USA but also in Australia, South Africa, France, Netherlands and South Korea.

Boeing 747-136 October 1973. Shown is another BOAC 747-136 G-AWNB taking off from LHR in May 1972.

Douglas DC10-30

The DC10 started as a series 10 aircraft which flew first on August 29th, 1970. This had a capacity of 270 passengers in two classes over a range of 3500 nmi. It entered airline service with American Airlines on August 5th, 1971.

The DC10-30 series was the same dimensions but made as a longer-range model to carry heavier weights, had a range of over 5200 nmi and a distinctive feature of a middle undercarriage bogie underneath the centre of the fuselage in order to carry the higher weights. 386 DC10's were built in all but the USAF also had a tanker version called a KC60 and 60 of these were built for them.

ZK-NZM was first flown on July 13th, 1973 and our flight was Auckland to Nandi on November 28th, 1973. It flew with Air NZ until 1982 when it went to American and continued with them until 2000. The last DC10 flight was in 2014.

Photo is of sister ship NZS on landing approach courtesy of Fred Barnes.

The DC10 had some problems in its career. The aft cargo door latches appeared locked but, in some instances, were not and American flight 96 over Windsor Ontario in June 1972 was lucky to survive the opening in flight and land safely.

Sadly, a Turkish flight Orly to Heathrow with full passenger load May 25th, 1974 as a result of the cargo door failing and heavy passenger load on floor above, deformed the floor to the extent all control cables were rendered useless and the aircraft crashed with total loss of life. Finally, the cargo door latches were remedied safe and the floor provided with vents.

An American Airlines flight out of O'Hare Chicago on May 25th, 1979, lost its left engine off the wing just after take-off which severed all hydraulics and the plane became totally uncontrollable and crashed with total loss of life. This grounded the DC10 worldwide until remedies could be found to fix the situation.

On a brighter note a United flight cruising from Denver to Chicago in July 1989 piloted by Capt. Al Haynes suffered a number 2 engine explosion (the tail mounted engine). A total hydraulic failure resulted and the crew with great airmanship skills used variable thrust on both their remaining wing engines to descend in circles and make an emergency landing in Sioux City Iowa.

Sadly, at the last minute on final approach the left wing was a little low and the aircraft went into a crash situation but despite the flames that you see on a video 184 survived but sadly 111 lost their lives.

There seem to be only two complete DC10 exhibits worldwide, one in Ghana and the other in Tucson but segments can be viewed in Manchester and Bali.

Douglas DC10-30 November 1973. ZK-NZS is shown courtesy of Fred Barnes.

Around Home

I'd had a difficult relationship with Anne's mother. While Anne was at home, she was part of the money earning process, and I don't think whether it was me or somebody else that took Anne away from mother's house and married her, it was going to be a big change to her mother's lifestyle which she didn't want to face.

She did move to a smaller place but there was some friction there for sure. Anyway, after some due consideration, Anne and I did decide to emigrate to NZ and in early 1974 started to put things in motion.

On the minus side, in late 1973, I'd just finished renovating my little Austin seven and got it on the road! I got about seven months of motoring out of it, drove it to a motor rally on the south coast once and generally had some good fun with it. Anne hated it and said it had no springs, but sadly when we leave UK in August 1974, I had to sell it! Photo here is Anne beside the car in the Thames valley area.

May 1974 The Austin seven now restored. Annie alongside it on a short afternoon excursion.

1974

March

Around now, the NZ government started to change the rules towards would be emigrants, so, we had to visit NZ Embassy in London, show them information about our house being for sale on real estate market etc. This granted us six months to enter NZ which I think gave us until end of September that year.

As you can imagine, Anne's mother was very opposed to our move and Anne assured her if she was in any trouble at all, she would come home and as it proved, was good to her word.

August the Move to NZ!

Things were very hectic right at the end in early August. We were in the house until the very last few days. I think we were both with BA (in glossary it explains both BEA and BOAC combined earlier on April 1st, that year) until only a week before we left.

Anne went to see her mother on the Wednesday night (we were due to leave on the Saturday) and was told she couldn't come in as she had a neighbour in for the evening. That was it!

Well Saturday, August 10th came, and we boarded a 747-100 G-AWNJ to JFK. I was so tired after all the action of the week, I was asleep after 45mins and I totalled up, of the nearly 26hrs we spent flying out to NZ, I was asleep for about 18 of them! On arrival JFK, we transferred onto a Standard VC10 (a new type for me so details are below).

About halfway on first sector JFK-LA, we negotiated through a storm front, and have included photo taken after we had passed into the clear air beyond. See the text book photo of the anvil head on the cumulonimbus cloud. Our cruise height was 35,000ft.

After one night in Nandi, we travelled on an Air NZ DC8 on August 12th, 1974 to 'The land of the Long White Cloud!'.

A text book anvil cloud seen out of the window of standard VC10 travelling JFK-LA at 35000ft August 1974.

Vickers Armstrong Standard VC10

The standard VC10 first flew on June 29th, 1962. The Super VC10 a stretched version carrying more passengers has been outlined earlier. The Standard was ideally suited to the Africa routes that BOAC operated which had high altitude airports with hot temperatures.

Of the 18 Standard VC10s built 12 went to BOAC with the remainder to a few other airlines and each carried around 109 passengers. The remainder of the 54 units built were super VC10s.

G-ARVM first flew on July 8th, 1964 and our flight was JFK-LA-Honolulu-Nandi, starting on August 10th, 1974 when it was owned by BA. This was the only time I flew on a Standard model. The interior cabin looked extremely short.

This plane stayed in service with BA until 1979 and was retained as a standby aircraft. After some moving around, the fuselage only, still remains as a museum exhibit at the Brooklands Museum, and I sat in it on a visit to UK in 2017.

Thanks to Gordon Reid for the photo. It was a take-off on an earlier sector Honolulu to Nandi in November 1969.

There are many complete Super VC10s on display in UK but one Standard which is G-ARVF on display in Germany.

Vickers Armstrong VC10 August 1974. Photo is same aircraft taking off in November 1969 Honolulu to Nandi and courtesy of Gordon Reid.

Getting Started in NZ

Well, there will be a bit of a personal story here. After a few nights in a motel after we first arrived, we managed to get the lease on the top floor of a house in a nice suburb called Remuera which is about 5 kms SE of Auckland city. Initially, I had an interview with Air NZ but could not be offered a position, so found a job in a travel agency to the south of Auckland.

I had only been there a matter of weeks and Air NZ called me and offered me a job in their Flight Crew rosters department, so I accepted that and the travel agency seemed to understand my situation, as my experience was more aligned to airline operations. So, by around mid-September, I was working for Air NZ and I think Anne had managed to obtain a position in Revenue Accounts also with the airline. So, we went into work together.

She was working on the 15th floor and I was on the 17th! With my previous skills as a draughtsman and building knowledge, I drew up plans for a house and we found a sizeable area of land to the NW of Auckland, some 15 Acres in fact, which we purchased.

So, we had enough money from our sale of the house in the UK to buy that land, and enough left to have what they term a shell, which looks to all intents and purpose from the outside to be a complete house, but needs to be fitted out totally inside. This type of house is built in a builder's yard and then transported by road in the early hours of the morning when traffic is light to the owner's plot.

1975

So, shell of the house was built early months of 1975 and put onto our plot in February. Now whilst I'd started working in Crew rosters, Ken a pilot who lived out in that area heard we were looking for somewhere to stay while we were finishing the inside of the house. Anne and I went out to meet Ken and Marnie, his wife, one evening and they seemed quite happy to take us in.

So, we left Remuera in early March and moved out to their place at Waitakere which is about 15 kms NW of the city and stayed with them for nine months.

Their house was just at the other end of the same road we were building in, so just two or three-minute drive time so very convenient for us.

They were such kind people and sometimes although I only speak to Ken about twice a year, it is like the last call was just yesterday when we get talking again!

So, my pattern during that nine months was every evening after work, up to work on the house for about 3 or 4hrs, and then the two days at the weekend. The house measured 900 square feet and maximum width had to be 20ft so it gets through bridges enroute hence the house was 45ft long. So just before Christmas 1975, I had finished the inside of our dwelling and we moved in!

The house we completed at Taupaki NW of Auckland. Around time we moved in December 1975.

1976

This started as a more settled year at least initially. We were in the house and getting more established. We only looked after the immediate surrounding area of the house. Around 14 of the acres we leased off to our neighbour who could use the land as extra for his own stock.

Anne was able to move from Air NZ and work for NAC reservations which suited her much better. We were still both working day jobs so could share the same car to and from the city.

June

Became a big turning moment for Anne. We returned home from work one evening in the early part of June and found a letter in the mailbox which was from one of Anne's mother's friends. She thought Anne should be made aware that her mother was in hospital and it was a serious condition, and gave details of the phone number of the hospital and the surgeons name etc.

It was only a matter of minutes before Anne had established contact with the hospital and the doctor who wasn't even aware his patient had a daughter! Anne's mother was suffering from terminal cancer, so although, it wasn't an immediate situation the prognosis was for only months of life, not more than that. The next morning, we arranged for Anne to leave on Air NZ via Papeete to LA then onto London.

Her mother was absolutely astounded when Anne walked into her hospital room, but Anne was as good as her word!

I'll complete this part of the story before I relate my own. Her mother did come out of hospital for a greater part of the next few months but she passed away at the end of August.

Anne after helping to tidy up affairs and empty the house in preparation for a sale, came back to NZ on around September 20th.

July to UK

My part in all this was that I felt I should be over there supporting Anne, so I took some leave and left Auckland on an Air NZ DC10 on July 7th via Papeete to LA. Flight was very full so Capt. Simpson out of Auckland kindly allowed me to occupy a flight deck jump seat to Papeete. There was more space in the cabin on the next sector to LA, so I was able to get a more comfortable seat for that sector which was 7hrs 34mins.

Because of night curfew in JFK, we had to wait in LA until later as we had to avoid a night landing at JFK. So, after a later take off from LA in a TWA (Trans World Airlines) 707 we transited JFK AM on 8th and travelled daylight to LHR arriving late evening local time.

I was able to spend two and a half weeks in the UK with Anne helping out as best I could, then I left on July 24th on a BA Super VC10, LHR to JFK. I was able to have one night there with my second cousin, Bettie (sister of Alice). Alice, by now, had retired from work and moved out of Manhattan and had retired up to Massachusetts.

Bettie lived in Westchester County around 45mins north of JFK on the mainland. Next day returning to the airport I get to fly on a new type a Lockheed 1011 to LA so details are as below. On arrival LA, I connected onto an Air NZ DC10 via Honolulu to Auckland. This time I'm back on NZM which was the first DC10 we flew on Auckland-Nandi back in November 1973.

Lockheed L1011 Tristar

This was Lockheed's entry to the wide body market and first flew November 16th, 1970, just around three months after the DC10, its main competitor. It carried 272 passengers as a typical load in a three-class layout and 250 units were built. Again, like the DC10 it had one engine mounted on each wing but the tail mounted engine was buried into the tail and fed by an S shaped intake duct the same as the Trident and 727 described earlier.

The DC10 was very different by having its engine straight through at the base of the tail. Eastern Airlines introduced the type into service on April 26th, 1972. Later a 500-series version had a reduced length fuselage and became a longer-range option of this aircraft.

N11003 photo is quite by chance the actual plane I flew on courtesy of Rob Finlayson. Aircraft was delivered to TWA on August 12th, 1972. My flight was from JFK to LA on July 25th, 1976.

Records appear to indicate it remained with TWA as it was still in their colours when put into storage at Kingman Arizona in July 1999. One Tristar is still in use as of August 2020 by Northrop Grumman as "Stargazer" assisting in astronomy observations.

Complete exhibits are available to view in at least five locations around the world in USA, France, UAE, Saudi Arabia and Trinidad.

Lockheed L1011 Tristar July 1976. This is the aircraft I flew on, photo courtesy of Rob Finlayson.

August to Hawkes Bay

Now I'm back in NZ and a bit lonely on my own out in the country, I headed down to see my brother for the weekend, so had Friendships flights down on August 6th, to Napier and came back on the 9th.

Changes in NZ

After Anne's return from the UK, she did return to NAC for a while but I had the offer of a move down to flight control in Air NZ which was in the same building but one floor down and involved shift work which I had been used to from my BEA days. It gave me greater pay so Anne resigned her NAC job and we managed on my one salary.

December to Papeete

In preparation for Christmas when my brother and his family of three kids were coming to stay with us, I knew Anne would need a break after the trying time she had experienced nursing her mother over in the UK, so we decided to take a break up to Tahiti and stayed at a resort out at the SE corner of the island called Tahiti-Iti.

It was Air NZ DC10's there and back from Auckland to Papeete return with ZK-NZP on December 3rd, on way out and on December 9th, NZM on the way back. NZP sadly was lost in the disastrous crash on the side of Mt Erubus in Antarctica some three years later in November 1979.

NZM keeps following me around that was my fourth flight! However, Tahiti was not the ideal place to go that time of year. It is supposed to be the rainy/off season. We were about the only people at the resort and though it started out fine, it soon turned to rain.

It was clear the resort considered us an interruption to their routine at that time of the year, and we came into the restaurant one evening and asked for Banana Fritters to be told there were none but there were bananas falling off the trees! We came back into Papeete but soon tired of being in Tahiti with incessant rain, so headed back to Auckland a few days early.

Instead of heading for home, had three nights left of my leave, drove south of Auckland to the Coromandel Peninsula and spent the weekend looking at beautiful beaches in brilliant sunshine with azure waters. Eat your heart out Tahiti!

1977

My parents came out to visit in 1977 in the early part of the year so sharing stays between my brother down in Napier which by the way is on the east coast of the North Island in NZ and ourselves in Auckland they could stay for around five months or so at a time but they also did tours as well and went down to the South Island on one. In May, they headed back to the UK.

My work continued in flight control during the year and Anne started to do voluntary work.

The 1st August, that year Amy, our daughter, was born! Well, that always changes your perspective on life and finances did come into it. In September, Pan American at Auckland Airport were advertising for two operations loadmasters, so I applied and was successful together with the other applicant, Brian, who had a background from NAC.

This gave me a big salary boost which was a real help. In Ramp operations for Panam at Auckland airport there would be two loadmasters on duty at a time. One would work in the office providing the flight crew with the flight plan and a prelim load sheet.

The other load master would be working out on the ramp by the aircraft with a chart of the holds, and supervising where each container or pallet would be loaded, and also where passengers would be loaded in appropriate zones in the cabin floor above to ensure the aircraft was within safe limits of CG (Centre of gravity) to ensure a safe take off and flight.

Initially, of course there was training to work through before I became qualified but by about November, I was working shifts as one of the team. There were early shifts and lates to contend with, but to meet a 747SP coming in from LA with an STA of 0600, I had to start at 4 AM and that meant up at three a bowl of cornflakes and out the door. It was a 45-min drive from NW of Auckland to the airport which is a bit to the south.

1978

July to Sydney

With me busy at the airport and Anne busy at home we move into 1978 and Panam send Brian and myself on a famil to Sydney. The details of the flights are below. Over was a Boeing 747SP. This was the most amazing plane! Before the arrival of the 747-400 over thirteen years later, this was an outstanding aircraft in what it achieved (and it looked very different too!).

It was the first truly long-haul airliner and a long way ahead in years of eventually what would follow! Brian and I were shown around the Panam facility which was much larger than our Auckland one, then overnighted and brought back to Auckland the following day on a 747-100F, the F standing for freighter.

The 100-series freighter (and the Combi) had a large Cargo door on the left-hand side in front of the tail which gave access to the main empty deck, which accommodated pallets and containers in two rows right down the length of the aircraft. It was quite a sight to see one of these planes empty. The Wright brothers would have been overwhelmed!

Boeing 747SP

This was developed from the 747 as a lighter longer-range option. It was unmistakable to look at, being so much shorter than the standard 747. In fact, it was shorter by 47ft!

The types first flight was on July 4th, 1975 and it began a new era in long haul flight. This aircraft was capable of flying San Francisco to Sydney non-stop! Panam ordered some to specifically cover the long hauls, such as the Pacific and New York to Tehran, and introduced them in 1976. Other airlines also purchased units but in relatively small numbers so total production of the SP was 45.

Initially, Panam's SPs were configured with 18 First, 62 Clipper class, and 164 economy for a total of 244 passengers but layouts varied between airlines and over the years of operation.

N534PA was accepted by Panam on May 28th, 1976 and my flight on this plane was Auckland to Sydney on July 10th, 1978. It continued flying with Panam until United purchased the Pacific routes and aircraft in February 1986. Thereafter, it continued flying with United still using the Panam flight numbers until it was withdrawn from service in March 1994.

In all I flew 12 SP sectors ten with Panam and mostly in the Pacific and trans-Tasman but included one Heathrow-LA sector plus two sectors on one of the Qantas SP's.

Photo is of N533PA courtesy of John Roach. I note that 5 of my 10 Panam sectors were flown on this airplane.

One survivor still in the air is former Panam 747SP N536PA which is now operated by NASA as "SOFIA" (see Glossary), and has a telescope on-board performing infrared astronomy.

The only SP I have found to date on view is at Rand airport in East Johannesburg in SAA (South African Airways) colours. There may be others.

Boeing 747SP July 1978. Shown is N533PA courtesy of John Roach.

Boeing 747-100F

The Boeing 747 also was designed not only to be a passenger airliner but to be a freighter, and the 100-series had a side loading door on the left side just forward of the tail. Later variants such as the 200-series also had a nose opening door which raised up to allow front loading. As mentioned earlier the first 747 flew on February 9th, 1969, but the first freighter flew on November 30th, 1971, and Lufthansa introduced them into airline service in April 1972.

Of the 176 100-series aircraft built, of these there does not seem to be an exact number of freighters that were produced but the numbers for later units are given below.

N654PA I flew on July 11th, 1978 from Sydney to Auckland as part of my Panam training.

This plane left the airline in 1983 and went to various operators finally with UPS (United Parcel Service) where it was still operating in 2002 as N682UP.

Photo is of sister ship N658PA, courtesy of Paul Seymour.

Many 747 freighters are still in use but mainly the later 200/300/400 series and the -8 model. The actual number that were built from those mentioned totalled 337 plus 13 convertible 200 models. Then added to this would be the number of 100-series which appear to be unknown.

There appears no record of any freighters on display but see October 1973 in this book for 747's that are in six various locations around the world.

Well, I'm sure you can all remember the most terrifying moment of your life, well here goes mine. I can't remember exactly when but it was during my four, otherwise happy years with Panam and each week it's a Tuesday when the freighter comes through from Sydney midday and transits Auckland on flight number PA872 then via Honolulu to LA.

So, each time it comes onto the chocks, my job if I'm the ramp Loadmaster, is once the stairs are positioned to the forward left door on the aircraft (door L1 we call it), is to board and walk down inside the plane to arrange the opening of the large cargo door down at the back. Now most of you can imagine as containers are rectangular and they are fitted into a round fuselage you will end up with some curious shapes around the containers.

At floor level, there is about 18 inches of walkway from the edge of the containers to the side of the fuselage, but at shoulder height that has probably widened out to 24 inches then tapers in of course higher up. As I'm walking down inside the aircraft, I get to some hessian covered weldmesh cages.

I notice the hessian is torn away so there is a hole, so as I get to opposite the hole a Lion's face jumps at me roaring at its most frightening with all its claws about 6 inches away from my face trying to get through the weldmesh! I don't know why Panam had the choice of a dark blue uniform but I think another colour might have been a good idea on that day!

We only know what position containers are coming off on the plan we receive from Sydney not what is in them. These were lions going to a Safari Park down in Christ Church. The Loadmaster nearly ended up in Auckland General with a cardiac arrest!

Life continued on through 1978. Luckily, I was still around to enjoy it!

Boeing 747-100F July 1978. Shown is N658PA courtesy of Paul Seymour.

1979

March to Sydney

Early in the year, we were contemplating a trip over to see my parents in the UK but thought it best to try out our daughter, Amy, on a flight. She was 20 months old when we set off to Sydney on a 747SP on March 31st.

It all went very well but I observed with younger children, shall we say infants, although Amy was getting past that stage, when the aircraft reaches the top of descent (TOD), the descent starts to increase pressure in the ears and tends to block off the hearing and then young babies fall asleep! That's my take on it anyway.

We had seven nights over there and showed Amy Taronga Zoo and called in to see Bill and Joyce, my second cousins, and other relatives who also lived there. Our trip back was another SP on April 7th, back into Auckland.

But one thing had started to trouble me, that Panam's flight 812, a daily 747 from Sydney via Auckland to Honolulu then LA was due to leave us at 9.55 PM (2155 to us lot). Well, it rarely did!

What was worrying, was that if it say left at 2300 or sometimes even later after coming in late from Sydney and going out an hour or so late, I would be leaving the airport sometimes as late as 1 AM and closer to home up the NW motorway it would be later than that, and an odd night I found myself nodding off at the wheel!

This had to be remedied! We, therefore, decided to make a move nearer the airport and we found a small cottage just to the west of Auckland.

It was in a beautiful village called Titirangi on the edge of hills that stretch up north called the Waitakere Range. Built in the 1920s, we were able to buy the cottage in 1979 for the princely sum of $22,000 which was money we had to hand.

So, we moved down from our NW Auckland home (the place name was Taupaki) and we rented that out. From Titirangi the drive was a comfortable

25mins to the airport and with quite a few intersections to keep me interested. I was safe on the roads once more.

The airport is on the fringes of the Manukau harbour and the rear views from our cottage looked out on the same harbour. It was on nearly a third of an acre and had thirteen Kauri trees on it. Truly a magnificent setting!

August to UK

We are heading off to London, leaving on the 20th on a 747SP to LA with flight time of 12hrs. Then connection on to a 747 LA to LHR arriving on the 21st with flight time of 9hrs 52mins. We spent time with my parents of course and my sister some 20 miles to the north, but also went up to the English/Scottish borders to see many relatives up there, plus to South Wales to visit Anne's relatives and friends.

We had one month in UK and left LHR on September 20th on an SP with flight time to LA of 10hrs 32mins. We had one night in LA before we moved on to Honolulu, the next day on an afternoon flight on a 747 so had three nights there. Big bonus was we had a hotel on the Esplanade and next morning after our arrival we were treated to the "Aloha Festival" which is celebrated by floats decorated in flowers parading past our kerbside viewpoint seemingly for an hour.

What an amazing spectacle! After the nights, we enjoyed there, we boarded another 747 early hours of 25th, with flight time of 8hrs 7mins arriving on 26th into Auckland having crossed the date line enroute. My flight log notes we had turbulence for half of that flight. It isn't always smooth up there!

Mum and dad visited New Zealand later in the year so to see them twice in the same year was just amazing. The jet age had certainly changed things for many families. They spend some time with us up in Auckland and then go down to see my brother in Napier, but always they came out for around five to six months to escape the worst of the UK winter.

1980

April to Sydney

We are now going to take a break and travel over to Sydney (again). It is a great place to visit, with many places to view and things to do. However, main purpose in the visit was mum and dad were still down in this part of the world having left NZ behind, and were staying in Australia before heading back to UK.

We therefore joined up with them and hired a car and drove up to the Gold Coast where we had access to a relative's apartment to stay at. After enjoying our stay up there we returned to Sydney and said our farewells and headed back to NZ. This was 747's both ways, westbound on the 1st April, and we spent 11 nights over there and returned on April 12th.

August to Honolulu

We had some leave and headed to Honolulu on August 5th, on a 747 with flight time of 7hrs 58mins. We had a great place to stay for seven nights just at the east end of the hotel strip and around the corner so it overlooked the park looking east towards the zoo and was only a six-storey building.

We did the usual tourist spots like Pearl Harbour Including USS Arizona but we also hired a car and went over to the east side of Oahu (called the Windward side) and got to visit several Panam cabin crew members who I had got to know through their trips to and from Auckland. We also did a tour right around the island although you can also sit on the local bus and do it for a very nominal fare!

After our Honolulu stay, we caught a Cessna 402 (details below) over to Maui on August 12th, and stayed there on the west coast for six nights. A great place to visit but I wish we had gone up to see some of the mountains as we had the hire car to do that, however we had Amy and at 3 years old, she was more interested in the paddling pool and the beach!

On August 18th, we flew back to Honolulu on an Aloha 737 (again details below) so in all there were two new types on this trip. We had two more nights in Honolulu and then left in the early hours of the 20th August, on another of Panam's 747's to Auckland, with a flight time of 8hrs 29mins arriving on August 21st.

Cessna 402A

This aircraft usually seated nine and is a useful plane for small regional operators. The type was first flown on August 26th, 1965 and one operator in the Caribbean in 2019 was still running a fleet of 88 of this type!

N4544Q the plane I flew on was built in 1969 and the flight was from Honolulu to Lanai a small island enroute then to Kaanapali on Maui on August 12th, 1980, the latter sector probably my shortest sector of the 454 flown at only 10mins! The airline had the flight prefix "ZH" and was called Royal Hawaiian Air Services. Registration on this plane was cancelled in 1980.

Cessna 402A August 1980. Shown is a sister ship courtesy of Howard Chaloner.

Boeing 737-200

This was a late starter in the twin jet short medium haul market, with its first flight on April 9th, 1967, over two years behind the DC9 for example but up to June 2020 they have sold close to 11,000 units!

The type first entered service with Lufthansa in 1968 and at that stage the 100/200 series passenger loads varied among airlines but were around 90-110 passengers, but typical Aloha seating was for 99. As the 300/400 series progressed, passenger loads increased to around 130-140, and with the 700/800, a load of 180 was quite typical. Sadly, the 737Max suffered a grounding and is a competitor to the Airbus A320NEO (New Engine Option) but has now returned to the air.

N70721 had been delivered to the airline on September 15th, 1977 and our flight was from Kahalui on Maui to Honolulu on Oahu on August 18th, 1980 for a flight time of just 20min (note that for the paragraph below). The plane went to Nigeria Airways in 1982 and after many more airlines ceased flying in Jun 2005. Photo below is after arrival Honolulu.

It's slightly ironic that my first 737 flight should have been on an Aloha 737 because of the tale that occurred to its sister ship, N73711. It had been delivered to Aloha in 1969 then had gone to another operator for a short time, but on its return and by April 28th, 1988 was flying at 24000ft from Hilo to Honolulu, when without warning 18ft of the cabin roof suddenly disappeared, sadly with the loss of one cabin attendant.

The aircraft with great skill from the two pilots managed to divert to Kahalui on Maui. The aircraft had done 35000 odd flying hrs which is not high for a 19-year-old aircraft, but what had 'fallen through the cracks', for want of a better expression, was that it had done the colossal number of 90,000 flight cycles which is around double what had been expected.

As you see from my flight above, we were in the air for only 20mins and if you take that number of cycles and work it out over nineteen years, it averages over 13 per day! It's all hindsight now but the inspection programmes were not in place at the time to account for such high cycles per day.

In all I've flown on 77 sectors on 737's! A great deal in Australia up and down the east coast of Australia, plus 16 around South Pacific including NZ, New Caledonia, Fiji and the Solomons plus four in the US, and five in Norway.

Boeing 737-200 August 1980. On arrival Honolulu.

1981

June to UK

We decided to have a trip to UK but I think there was writing on the wall that Panam were in the decline and that some staff layoffs were inevitable. As I was one of the last hires in 1977, it was possible I would be one of the first to go! I was assured there would be a job for me in the airline even if it wasn't in Operations.

Anyway, in early June, Anne and Amy went ahead to London and spent time in Cornwall and South Wales seeing friends and relatives of Anne's while I worked onto mid-June. I left on June 17th on a new type a Qantas 747-100 Combi (see details below) from Auckland to Sydney, had one night with Bill and Joyce, then went on with BA on a 747-100 via Kuala Lumpur-Abu Dhabi-London.

My seat was right over the wing so heard a tyre blow on landing at Abu Dhabi but to show how professional the engineering staff are, we left for LHR one minute early! So, I met up with Anne and Amy at LHR (Amy now coming up to 4 years of age) and saw my parents and all the usual relatives down south and up north.

So, for me after twenty-one nights UK, we left on July 11th from LHR to LA but Panam were so full, we had to take a seat on a BA 747-200 a new type for me (see details below), but we only boarded with cabin baggage. We had too much baggage for BA to carry it, but as I worked for Panam they would carry our bags to LA. This just DOESN'T happen now!

As soon as we had our boarding passes for BA, I went back to the Panam desk and they released the bags onto their flight.

Now I'll try to give you the brief version. Once you clear customs in LA, you cannot go back in to the customs hall and claim your bags which were coming in on a different arrival hub. I had to collect them the next morning at a kerbside claim point (we had planned to stay a night in LA anyway). Next morning, I claimed two bags of seven (five had been tagged to go straight through to

Auckland) which all had heavy clothes in, which we didn't need for Honolulu, our next destination.

Got back to the hotel with what I thought were the right bags but they certainly felt heavy, and Anne took one look called me a lot of things including "raving idiot" and I had tagged the wrong bags completely! Flight to Honolulu was late that day so we hired a car, went via shopping mall, got some beach wear and a few other bits and got back to the airport to check-in.

What happens next is beyond belief but flight is full and we don't get on but our bags DO!

We have really missed our chance of a worthwhile stop in Honolulu, so we go back down to the car hire depot only a few hours after we had left it, get another car, drive up to Santa Barbara for three nights, and next day buy some more beach wear! There is an SP going down non-stop to Auckland on night of July 15th which we board with a flight time of 12hrs 8 mins, to find all seven bags waiting for us in the Ops room!

Boeing 747-238 Combi

Qantas obtained three combi aircraft which had the cargo door at the aft end of the main passenger deck, so it could handle a number of pallets in roughly the rear third of the plane, and forward of a bulkhead there was a normal cabin of seats but carrying a reduced passenger load. The plane I flew on had Pratt and Whitney power but the other two Qantas Combis were Rolls Royce RB211 powered.

VH-ECA first flew on October 4th, 1977 and operated its first service for Qantas on October 29th, 1977.

My flight was Auckland to Sydney on June 17th, 1981. It finished operating for Qantas in August 1987 and went to Air Canada with tail number 308 and ceased flying with them in 1999.

Photo is courtesy of David Carter. The top of the cargo door opening is just discernible in the image. Also note that, although, the 5th door on the left side is there (called L5 in aviation terms), it is not highlighted as doors one to four are, as there is only cargo behind it, hence no need for passenger evacuation through that door or immediate assistance from outside rescuers.

I later flew on an Air Canada Combi tail number 307 Heathrow-Bombay (now Mumbai)-Singapore in January 1989.

I'm not aware of Combi's on display but refer October 1973 in this book for locations of 747's in various countries.

Boeing 747-238 Combi June 1981. Photo courtesy of David Carter.

Boeing 747-200

Basic details of the 747 have been outlined earlier (see October 1973 in the book) but the 200-series improved over the 100 with better range, higher take-off weight and most were fitted with ten windows per side on the upper deck allowing for better use of the upper area. The type was introduced into airline service in February 1971.

My first flight on the 200 model was from Heathrow to LA on BA's G-BDXJ on July 11th, 1981. In fact, BA used economy seats in the upper deck which is where we were seated.

This plane went onto other operators later, and was withdrawn from service in February 2004. Photo is courtesy of Fred Barnes.

In all I flew on ten 200 series sectors but one was on G-BDXH in 1988. See the story later in the book. See October, 1973 for 747's on display around the world in museums.

Boeing 747-200 July 1981.
Here G-BDXC is shown on approach to LHR courtesy of Fred Barnes.

July

Even after arriving back in Auckland from above trip my boss met me and assured me, I would still have a job somewhere in the airline. However, just before we left for the trip, I had notice from the property we had moved into, as Anne had not been happy with the cottage, so we were renting a modern Lockwood home still with lovely views of the Manukau Harbour, but they needed their home back ASAP.

So the afternoon we arrived back, we headed to a real estate company handling rentals and started visiting properties. By next day, we had found a suitable one nearby and moved over there by the weekend!

I'd returned to work but was at home early the next week, when my boss, Tim, called me and said regretfully, I did not have a job with Panam anymore as from mid-September, and he was basically as upset about the handling of the matter as we were. They did, after my protests, give me some severance pay so that meant I really needed to look for fresh aviation work.

Oddly enough, at the time an ex-BEA Vickers Viscount G-AOHT (I won't tell you what we called that one!) had come out to NZ and was in the colours of a proposed private airline called 'Skybus', where club members would purchase a ticket for a set amount of dollars and it would ply the trunk routes of Auckland-Wellington-Christchurch.

However, the Attorney General came into the fray at the last moment and ruled that the passengers would not have suitable public liability. This in a country that had been known to have Jewellers open on a Sunday selling oranges for $300 and giving away free diamond rings!

Two things happened here, I asked my parents if they would like to come out whilst I was still with Panam which they said they would, and they came out late August, and travelled out with my sister's daughter, Sue, just turned 17. They stayed with us initially and then went down to my brothers in Napier. I left Panam in mid-September, but the airline still gave me a generous period to resettle.

September to Sydney Fact Finding

As Skybus had been shelved, we decided I should seek work in Australia so headed to Melbourne on Panam's 747 on September 16th. I had interviews with TAA (Trans Australia airlines) and Ansett Airlines whilst I was over there. Then on 17th, I travelled on Ansett 737 to Sydney and had two nights with Bill and Joyce, then on 19th, an Ansett 727 to Brisbane where I met up with Anne and Amy who had flown in from Auckland.

After two nights, there it was an Ansett 737 back to Sydney. Now Panam said they had a bit of disruption and best plan for us was to head to Melbourne and fly with them next day, from there back to Auckland. So as ordered, we flew down on their 747 to Melbourne and stayed the night.

Well as they say, the best laid plans of mice and men! What comes next you can guess. We fly home from Melbourne on an SP on September 23rd but it takes us back up via SYDNEY! To Auckland!

We do a second trip to do more fact finding later in the year.

Later September

After our return from Australia, we headed down to Rotorua which is a good half way meeting point for my brother's family and ours plus there were our parents plus Sue out from UK. Quite a family get together!

October to Honolulu

Around this time, Sue needs to head back to the UK and we give her a helping hand and escort her the first part of the journey up to Honolulu. We leave on Panam 747 on October 12th, fairly quick time of 7hrs 49mins. We see Sue off on connecting flight via Seattle to London.

Over the years with Panam, I have made friends with a number of the cabin crew based in Hawaii and were invited to stay with one hostess. The husband was away on business so it was only our friend, Tu, the Panam employee at home, so we had initially a good time together but she was on standby and did get called in for duty. No big deal.

We ended up care taking for their eight cockatoos ranging right up to the largest Hyacinth Macaw! What a magnificent bird but we hadn't expected that, but it was an interesting experience!

After eight nights, we caught another 747 back early hours of the 20th October, with flight time of 8hrs 7mins to Auckland.

November to Sydney More Fact Finding

We had decided to head for Australia to live in the near future so thought we would take a longish trip to check out a few things. We had previously taken my parents up to the Gold Coast in SE Queensland, when they were on a stay in Australia and we travelled over from Auckland to join them. We were impressed with the area so thought it worth a revisit considering moving away from airline work and living up there.

At the same time, in any case there were two airports, one on the Gold Coast which had in the main domestic flights down to Sydney and Melbourne but Brisbane airport was only about 100 kms to the north. Anyway, we purchased a Holden panel van to use on this trip which we could leave at the workplace of one of my cousin's husbands on our return back down to Sydney whilst we returned to Auckland to wind up our affairs there.

Flight over was November 23rd, on a 747SP and back on a 747 on December 7th.

At home in Auckland, I had time on my hands being unemployed for the first time, basically other than when moving countries, so I helped out a friend doing renovations on his house, and finished working on a fibreglass bodied car based on a Triumph Herald Chassis which I had been working on for some time. I got this on the road in NZ and brought it over to Australia and used it there for a few years.

1982

February to Sydney One Way!

Today is my last flight with Panam, and I still have nickname of "Abe" as continuing reminder of my time with the airline. I'd been very happy with Pan American. It had been a great team to work for and I still look back at those days with fond memories.

I'm fairly tall and sport a beard and working with American pilots on a daily basis it wasn't long until the nickname of "Abe" had been duly given. That had continued through my other airport work which comes later.

March Settling in on the Gold Coast

I had come over on my own and after time in Sydney with Bill and Joyce, duly made my way up to the Gold Coast, this time by surface in preparation to meet Anne and Amy plus our cat who arrived into Brisbane in early March.

After a few nights at a motel, we found a duplex (a semi-detached single dwelling) to rent and this was in a place called Burleigh Waters, quite near the famed Burleigh Heads, which is a renowned scenic spot on the middle of the Gold Coast complete with rainforest walks on the headland overlooking the ocean.

Around June, I was able to get work as a handyman come gardener. Some of the time, I was working on the owner's boat usually two days per week at Southport Yacht Club, and the rest of the time at his house to the rear of Surfers Paradise. That work lasted until September the next year.

Meanwhile on the house front, we found a one acre plot about 10 kms back from the sea which was elevated, and offered coast views, and we purchased that early on and put plans into council, which were approved and found a builder to start construction.

Sadly, as with all my projects I never seem to have the money to do the whole thing, so as per NZ, around August had a 'shell' which I needed to finish off inside, which took the rest of the year to finish but we moved in for Christmas!

I had been looking for airline work without success, but during this time of doing handyman work, did attend courses in Brisbane for a Qantas sponsored Fares and Ticketing course, which is what you would basically need if you were to run a travel agency.

1983

Middle of this following year, I'm doing handyman work and travelling home one night through a village a few kms to the north of us, I noticed a large building being built with a bank to go in plus other retail shops. This village called Mudgeeraba already had 25 retail shops and on looking elsewhere, this seemed to be the point where there should be at least one travel agent in the centre, so we made the decision to open our own agency, which basically became quite successful.

October, Travel Agency Opens

"Horizon Travel" opened after I had done all the shop fitting myself, so the outlay to get started was very minimal. It became a successful business even with some opposition moving in at a later date, and we sold it fourteen years later as a going concern in October 1997!

1984

Early this year, I had booked my parents on a round the world ticket, so they visited USA first, then NZ and came to us finally on their way back to the UK, and stayed from April, until June. Sadly, it turned out it was the last time I was to see my father alive but more of that later.

1985 and 1986

Well this brought us down to earth with a bump running our own business! No paid leave, turn up for work every day. I think the general population think that it's all trips away in a travel agency. It might be in the very large ones, when one person at a time can easily be sent away on an agent famil or the Manager can go to the groups AGM etc.

This doesn't work in the small agencies where it is one or two people starting it up. Initially, for about the first three years, we had no computers so every booking was done by phone and tickets were mailed to us. Eventually American Airlines who sponsor an airline reservation system called "Sabre" based in Tulsa, had a promotion to encourage smaller agencies access and we finally got online with Sabre in 1986, which made life so much easier.

By then, we had joined a travel group called UTAG (United Travel Agent Group) which gave us better buying power with Tour wholesalers, than being totally stand-alone, but also gave us the opportunity to network with other agents and exchange ideas and benefits, generally from knowledge within the Industry.

1987

March to Sydney

It was now I started to get invitations through UTAG and from Airlines to go on either weekend workshops or famils. The first was a TAA weekend workshop down to Sydney for only the one night away on TAA's 737's. The only added excitement on this was a diversion coming back due to a severe thunderstorm at our local airport Coolangatta (now called Gold Coast airport), so we landed in Brisbane, spent an hour and a half there and then had a 15min flight back to our home airport.

April to Hamilton Island

Following month, Ansett took us up to Hamilton island in the Whitsunday Group of Islands half way up the Queensland coast with 737's both ways, and we spent one night on Hamilton, and then launch over to South Molle island for a further night.

A really nice trip but Catamaran on the way back was rough to Hamilton airport, and hitting a cross channel of water a side window shattered with the impact of water and the unfortunate adjacent passenger was admitted to Hamilton island hospital. I hate those boats and I've had three really rough rides in them!

December to Lady Elliott Island

My sister, Elaine, and her husband, Brian, were on a trip down-under from UK and visited us first before travelling onto NZ. We drove up to Bundaberg, about 5hrs' drive north of Brisbane, which is a jumping off point for Lady Elliot island a coral atoll which is the most southerly on the Great Barrier Reef. Travel over was December 12th on a new type (details are below) and we had two nights there before returning back from the island to Bundaberg and driving back south.

These islands are magical places to visit, and turtles come ashore November, and December, to lay eggs in the sand which hatch in the January–February period. That's a great time to visit and try and include a full moon around your dates and you'll thank me forever!

Britten-Norman BN-2 Islander

Originally, this partnership of John Britten and Desmond Norman were building Hovercraft in the 1950s, but a decade later, they could see the need for a small rugged regional airline aircraft which could serve several different purposes. They designed this nine passenger fixed undercarriage aircraft which first flew from Bembridge on the Isle of Wight in UK on June 13th, 1965. Since then, 1280 have been built and around 750 are still in active service!

Our flight on VH-FCO took place on December 12th, 1987 from Bundaberg in Queensland 50 miles out to Lady Elliot Island an Island Atoll on the Great Barrier Reef where an airstrip runs across the width of the island. This plane continued flying with this operator until 1992 then to various others and was still in use in Fiji in 2003.

In all I've flown six Islander sectors, three on the Lady Elliot route, one in Fiji, and two in NZ.

A development of this plane was called the Trislander which had a third engine installed towards the top of the fin. It was, therefore, able to carry a far bigger payload and was a much bigger size overall than its smaller sister but only 72 were built.

Britten-Norman BN-2 Islander December 1987. On arrival Lady Elliot Island.

1988

January

When my sister, Elaine, and husband returned to UK in early New Year, they were confronted by a serious family situation. My father who they knew was receiving treatment for Leukaemia had been admitted to hospital but my mother who admittedly hadn't seemed that well when they left in November, was also in the same hospital with terminal cancer!

My brother in NZ decided to fly over and took long service leave and left on January 20th, and on arrival helped give Elaine support in the situation. I was kept informed about how things were going. We then move on a few days.

26 January, was Bi-Centennial Day in Australia, so I was enjoying a lie in bed and it was my brother calling from UK saying on the Monday evening, that just before he had left the hospital, our dad was responding to the treatment, and that the doctors were forecasting two years of life ahead for him. So, I enjoyed the day and saw two RAAF (Royal Australian Air Force) F111's fly past Burleigh Heads from our vantage point in our street, and retired to bed at night where upon the phone rang again.

My brother had returned to the hospital the next morning, over there to find our dad had passed away! That really was a shock!

To UK

By Thursday, January 28th, I was on an SQ (Singapore airlines) 747-200 to Singapore and transferred onto an SQ "Big top" 747-300 (see details below). I was limited in time away, so was able to attend my father's funeral which was held in the hospital chapel, so that my mother could be there together with my brother and sister.

Then helped my brother at my parents' house to tidy up some things of dad's before I had to return to Australia, and mum came out of hospital to come home on the very day I departed. That was the hardest farewell I ever had to do!

I left on an SQ 747-300 LHR—Singapore-Brisbane. Usually, there is an aircraft change in Singapore but in this instance the same plane operated both sectors. All the 747-300's were American registrations.

BOEING 747-300

This was a further development of the 747 with extended range, more powerful engines and the major difference being an extended upper deck by just over 23ft. This and the 400 that followed had the same basic shape. They now featured a straight staircase to the upper deck compared to the spiral one of the 100 and 200-series planes. The 300 took to the air for the first-time on October 5th, 1982, and first delivery was to Swissair in March 1983.

Typical seating on 300 and later on the 400-series was generally 416 in three classes.

My first flight on this type was on N124KK, although, a US registration, it was operated by SQ and it was on January 28th, 1988 starting from Singapore via Dubai to LHR. SQ took delivery of this plane three years previously on September 24th, 1985.

It moved to other airlines in December, 2000 and into storage in 2007.

In all I flew on ten sectors on the 300 model either with SQ or Qantas.

SQ called the 300-series aircraft "Big Tops". A typical sector of 12hrs could be achieved and westbound from Singapore to London a stop at Dubai, or some other point would be needed for fuel but London-Singapore eastbound was usually achievable. Flight time on this particular return journey non-stop on February 9th, 1988 was 12hrs 9mins. It wasn't until the 400-series was introduced in 1989 that we had a large airliner that was truly long haul.

Boeing 747-300 January 1988. Photo kindly provided by Rob Finlayson for a sister ship for this type.

February

After my return, it was very difficult to adjust back to work knowing that my mother only had a short time left, but at least my brother and sister were both there, so that gave me a great comfort. My mother got re-admitted to another hospital mid-February, and she rallied a little when she realised my sister's birthday was coming up on the 27th of the month but then passed away on the 29th.

It just wasn't possible for me to return again to the UK for her funeral and I'm sure she would certainly have expected me to carry on and make my business as successful as I could make it. I still wonder at losing two parents in the space of five weeks. I guess it's fairly rare unless it happens both pass together in a road accident or similar.

September to Sydney

Work continued through the year, and there was a two-night UTAG famil down to Sydney on 23rd, returning on the 25th. The aircraft were both Qantas. Going down was a new type a Boeing 767-200 (see details below) and a 747-200 on the return. Both from Brisbane and returning there.

Boeing 767-200

This was a second-generation wide body jet together with the 757 and other Airbus products of the time. It was a medium to long haul plane which first flew on September 26th, 1981 and entered service with United in September the following year. A typical full passenger load of 216 in two classes could be carried over 3900 nmi but a reduced number of 181 could be carried over nearly 6600nmi.

The 300-series was over 21ft longer and introduced by Japan Airlines in 1988, could carry up to 269 over the 3900 nmi and reducing the number to 218 could attain a range of nearly 6000 nmi. Boeing have built 1223 units of the 767 and as at 2018, 742 of them were still in service.

VH-EAO was the first of my 767 rides and was a 200-model belonging to Qantas and was a short sector of only 468 miles from Brisbane to Sydney on September 23rd, 1988. In all I flew on 21 sectors on 767s, some short, some long haul with Air NZ, SAS, Australian and many of them with Qantas. All of the Qantas planes whether 200 or 300 were extended range versions. Aircraft photo is EAJ again kindly provided by Rob Finlayson.

There is one 767-200 purchased and restored by the employees of Delta and called "The Spirit of Delta" and is in their museum at Atlanta USA.

Boeing 767-200 September 1988. Shown is VH-EAJ courtesy of Rob Finlayson.

November to UK

As this had been an unusual year with both my parents passing so close together, Anne and I discussed going back to the UK to be with my sister on this occasion. It felt the right thing to do and we bought revenue fares because that time of year, there had to be a certainty that you would get on the flights! We left on November 26th, Brisbane to Honolulu on a Qantas 747-200 and connected there to a sister ship to LA.

There was a week in LA staying at Anaheim seeing Disneyland and travelling up to Hollywood to see Universal Studios, also over to Long beach to tour Queen Mary and see Howard Hughes Spruce Goose. It was a warm week, especially when thinking it was leading into December. Then we taxied out on December 1st, on a BA 747-200 at LA for the flight to LHR and I thought how 'tired' the aircraft looked! The following story might tell you why!

Earlier in June 1982, this aircraft with Capt. Eric Moody in command was in cruise over Indonesia on a flight down to Perth and around 180 kms SE of Jakarta the four engines flamed out! The captains' announcement was one of the coolest, "We have a small problem. All four engines have stopped and we are doing our damnedest to get them going again. I trust you are not in too much distress!"

The aircraft had flown through a volcanic ash cloud which as it's made of dry particles does not show up on weather radar. Fortunately, with the engines out, the silica which had built up on the turbine blades cooled, solidified and broke away, and at lower altitude the crew managed to get all four engines restarted and diverted to Jakarta.

They didn't see too much on approach as the cockpit glass was pretty opaque! In airline circles the aircraft named "City of Edinburgh" became affectionately dubbed "City of Jakarta"! From this, a valuable lesson was learnt and anything related to volcanic activity is well monitored and ash clouds avoided by aircraft when necessary. Each year the passengers and crew assemble to rejoice in life and meet up with each other!

On arrival LHR next day, we stopped overnight with Ron, an old friend of mine from BEA days, before we headed off down to Cornwall. In passing I happened to mention we had just come in on 'DXH' and then he advised us the relevance of the plane we had just been on. I was well aware of the "Mayday" flight, but didn't know it was this aircraft. Probably better finding out after we had landed!

We had over a month in UK, starting from Cornwall seeing the normal round of friends and relatives on both sides of our families, but especially remember arriving in the area close to my sisters prior to Christmas and seeing every TV screen filled with pictures of PA103 and its crash into Lockerbie in SW Scotland.

I cannot recall having met the flight deck crew because there were so many but I'm sure they would have been through Auckland at some time during my years earlier in the 1980s. More about Lockerbie later see January 2016.

We spent a very enjoyable Christmas at my sisters but our stay was then coming to a close.

1989

January

Early in the New Year on the 7th of January, we left LHR via Mumbai to Singapore.

This time on an Air Canada 747-200 Combi. I've rated this first sector as one of my fastest flights, although, BOAC in May 1966 gets first prize! Flight time from London to Mumbai with a very strong tail wind was only 7hrs 50 mins and for a distance of 4469 miles, that's an average speed of 570 mph.

Again, this was a very hard worked airplane but Air Canada certainly made up for it with the quality of their cabin service. Most impressive!

We had a week in Singapore seeing the sights, and then caught a ferry from the town of Changi at the east end of the island to the southern tip of Malaysia and went to a resort on the east coast called Desaru for around three nights. The ferry trip over was a bit of a worry in what looked like a small 20ft-long leaky boat but it did have what seemed to be a bright brand-new diesel engine sitting in the middle which gave some degree of reassurance.

We went back via taxi! At the causeway at the very southern tip of Malaysia at Johor Bahru, we had to change from a Malay taxi to a Singaporean one for the rest of the journey to Changi airport.

We left Singapore on January 17th, on a Qantas 747-200 but around 3hrs late for which we hadn't been advised of a delay, although, it was due to a late incoming aircraft. Flight time back to Brisbane was 6hrs 34mins, which was fairly quick.

1990

February to Fiji

On February 7th, I was invited to travel on a famil to Fiji. Departure was on a Fiji registered aircraft DQ-FDM, a 737-200 but in the colours of Solomons Airlines. On this schedule, the flight operated via Port Vila in Vanuatu to arrive in Nandi in the Fiji Islands. From there we connected onto a Britten Norman islander (first trip was one to Lady Elliot in 1987) to Malolo Lailai Islands about 20 miles west of Nandi where we stayed for two nights at Plantation Island Resort.

Following that we took a fast launch NE visiting other islands such as Treasure Island and Beachcomber before arriving on the NW of main Island Viti Luvu from where we were bussed down to the Coral Coast half way from Nandi eastward towards Suva the Capital. We stayed two nights at the Shangri-La Hotel resort but it's not all relaxation!

The main aim on famils seems to be to show so many resorts and room types that you get resort blur. I think most of us did. But we had a good time as well!

Finally, on February 11th, we bussed back west to Nandi airport and then reboarded FDM but this time non-stop back to Brisbane flight time 3hrs 34mins.

April to Solomons

Another famil! This to a really impressive destination one I would like to revisit. On April 26th, again we were on 737 FDM but this time Brisbane to Honiara the capital of the Solomon Islands.

After one night in Honiara, we were flown out in a Twin Otter (see details at foot of this segment). Affectionately they are called 'Twotters'. The first sector westbound was to an island called Seghe, where once landed, we took a short walk down to a jetty and were transferred by small launch over the Marovo lagoon, which is the second largest saltwater lagoon in the world to Eupi, an island resort for a one-night stay.

After exploring the small island, next day early we were returned to Seghe for an onward flight west to Munda and then Gizo. The check-in facilities at Seghe is a wicker hut where a panel on the side is held up by a broomstick when check-in is in progress! I think you get the picture. What comes next is quite entertaining.

One of our party had been in this area before and knew some of the ropes, so talked the natives into shinning up the coconut trees and getting some nuts down for us to drink from. See the photo below. Just as well it wasn't a DC10 that had landed! I think Munda is incorporated into the schedules as a fuel stop.

Flight time to Munda was 17mins. Then onto Gizo only 15 mins more. At Gizo, this is a main diving centre in the west of the Solomons and we stayed out of the town in an elevated position in a diving lodge. During that time, we were taken out by launch to "Plum Pudding Island" where John Kennedy and his men got marooned and then they all swam to another island some distance away which had water and food before their rescue.

Back in Gizo it was Sunday and the singing in church as we passed it, seemingly was about to raise the roof! What a joyful sound! We then headed back from Gizo through Munda to Honiara. Munda had its story.

The crew said we had 15mins so we all walked into the bar in the terminal, but most got back to the plane around 12mins later. We were taxiing away but the crew hadn't done a head count and two people were running alongside pounding on the door! We stopped and pulled them in!

Munda during WW2 had a very long runway of around 3000 m but after the end of the war, the need for such a long runway was not necessary and looking down the length in 1990 only about half was visible before jungle overtook the remaining half. Nowadays it has been reopened to some extent to be available as a suitable alternate for international jets requiring to divert from Honiara.

All five of our Twotter sectors in the Solomons were the same aircraft but I think there were at least two planes with the airline at the time. After our return to Honiara, we were bussed east of there to a coastal resort but I think this lacked some of the appeal of the western resorts and after one night there it was back to the airport for the flight home to Brisbane again on 737 FDM on April 30th.

De Havilland Canada DHC6 (Twin Otter)

This airplane is a rugged 19 passenger STOL (Short Take Off Landing) performance aircraft. The type was first flown May 20th, 1965 and to date 985 have been built and they have turboprop power. More recently ownership of the build is now performed by Viking Air.

It is used for commuter airlines but many of these aircraft will be found in outback places operating on grass strips, on skis doing snow landings and many operate on floats. Vancouver harbour is a busy place for them!

H4-SIB was registered in the Solomons in 1987 and my first sector of five was on April 27th, 1990, from Honiara the capital, west to the island of Seghe (a grass strip across the island). Distance was 159miles and flight time was 1hour 6mins. This plane was finally withdrawn from use in 2001.

Airport refreshments "Native style" at Seghe island
Solomon Islands April 1990

Other than the five sectors flown on this plane in the Solomons, I flew two sectors on a BA aircraft in 2008 in the Western Isles of Scotland.

De Havilland Canada DHC6 Twin Otter April 1990. On arrival Seghe in Solomons.

October to Japan

Another famil for the year. By way of explanation the business has been growing and we have a full-time consultant on our staff named Betty, a very experienced lady, so even if Anne and I were away at the same time she would be capable of running the office!

This time Japan Airlines have asked me away together with around seven others. So, we board a DC10-30 (same type as Air NZ fly) leaving Brisbane on October 15th, with flight time 8hrs 18mins to Narita Tokyo.

We stayed in Tokyo for three nights seeing various hotels and sights and then moved down to Kyoto on our first Bullet train (called Shinkansen) for two nights to see hotels there and temples and shrines. Also, did a day trip to Hiroshima to visit the Peace Museum and a ferry over to Miya Jima Island. A very thought-provoking day to visit Hiroshima.

For our last night we went east, again on Bullet train to Nagoya where we changed onto a more normal slower train into the Japanese Alps to Takayama and stayed in a traditional Ryokan for one night. Most of the tour group went down the next morning to the train station for a western breakfast, but I stuck it out with our tour guide and had Japanese style which I think was raw eggs and rice. When in Rome I say!

It was just a little early to see the autumn leaves in full glory but they were changing here and there so I was able to capture it on some of my photos.

We left Takayama October 21st, down to Nagoya then the Shinkansen (though they have faster ones now) to Tokyo then out to Narita for a DC10 flight home, time 8hrs 30mins arriving morning of the 22nd into Brisbane.

December to NZ

We decided to head to NZ for Christmas to spend with my brother and family. Anne and I were going to travel Business Class. Question for Amy, our daughter. Did she want to go with us up front or travel in economy and have the difference in spending money? She took the spending money!

We had brought her up right after all! We left from Brisbane on December 20th, on an AIR NZ 747-200 to Auckland and after a night there, spent a night with Ken and Marnie now living in Tauranga in the Bay of Plenty, Ken having retired from flying with Air NZ. We then had two nights further towards my brothers at Lake Waikaremoana a delightful spot in the middle of the north island SE of Rotorua.

Finally, we arrived at my brothers place on Christmas eve, and after a great Christmas, we added their daughter, Gail, into our car and gave her a lift down to Wellington. After a couple of nights there, on January 1st, we took the ferry over Cook Straight to Picton at the top of the South Island and picked up a fresh car hire.

We travelled down the west coast, walked on the Fox Glacier, then through Haast Pass to Queenstown, visited Milford Sound and finally returned to Christchurch for our flight home.

When we checked-in Air NZ, saw that we were in Biz Class but as economy was very full, upgraded Amy to travel with us! She got her money and half the perks!

15 January 1991, was the trip back to Brisbane on an Air NZ 767 flight time 3hrs 21mins.

1991

August to Hong Kong

This month I attended a UTAG AGM in Hong Kong. Initially on August 16th, I departed Gold Coast Airport (was Coolangatta) on a TAA 727-200 down to Sydney and stayed one night with Bill and Joyce. Next day up to Hong Kong with my first ride on a 747-400 (see details below) landing at the old Kai Tak airport.

After the AGM and its activities which takes around two days, I extended my stay and toured Hong Kong Island, the south coast of which had exclusive homes in manicured gardens very reminiscent of those on lakeside shores in Italy or the south French Riviera. I returned on night of August 22nd, on another Qantas 747-400 this time non-stop into Brisbane flight time 7hrs 58mins.

Boeing 747-400

Well finally I get to ride on what turns out to be the ultimate version of the 'Queen of the Skies'! The 400 series was an improved version of the 300 but with more powerful engines, higher take-off weight, it featured winglets on the end of the wings, which clearly now identifies it from the 300 and has a range of 7285 nmi.

Typical passenger layout is basically unchanged at 416 in three classes although as first class in modern days became lie flat, passenger numbers tended to come down a little. Of the 1564 747s built, 694 have been 400-series aircraft. The 400 model first took to the air April 28th, 1988 and entered service with North West in February, the following year.

VH-OJC operated its first Qantas service from Heathrow through to Sydney on October 12th, 1989.

My flight was from Sydney to Hong Kong on August 17th, 1991.

Its last service was a Sydney-LA flight on March 11th, 2014. It has now returned to Australia and is now on display in the HARS museum (Historical Aircraft Restoration Society) in NSW.

In all I flew on 14 sectors on the 400-series and some of them only Sydney to Brisbane but mainly long haul, one a Malaysian plane leased to Air NZ, Also Air NZ, Thai and SQ.

The photo shows VH-OEJ which at one stage had been painted in the red Aboriginal themed 'Wunala Dreaming' colour scheme, a true spectacle wherever it went in the world. This photo was taken on one of its last flights on a tour round Australia flying past the Gold Coast in southern Queensland.

A few days later on July 23rd, 2020, it departed Sydney for LA on its sad farewell but not without depicting in the sky a very cleverly patterned 'roo' which showed on flight radar map some 100 miles high! A great send off to an amazing plane!

With COVID in 2020 most airlines were painfully aware the economics of new runners in the market even Boeings own 777 and 787 plus Airbus A350 were detracting from 747s bottom line and most airlines were to phase them out in the next few years but the pandemic just accelerated the progress and has basically brought to a close fifty years of aviation history.

For other 747s on display see the listing given October 1973 earlier in the book.

Boeing 747-400 August 1991. Shown is VJ-OEJ last remaining Qantas 400 series prior to leaving for USA in July 2020. Earlier this aircraft known as "Wunula Dreaming" was painted in a striking Aboriginal Colour scheme.

1992

March to Bali

This time a tour wholesalers famil to Bali, departed from Brisbane March 18th on a Qantas 747SP (they had two of this type in their fleet) to Denpasar. We had two nights in Kuta which is where most people going to Bali stay, or at least on that coast which heads up the west coast from near the airport.

After seeing the normal range of hotels, we headed over to Nusa Dua, which is a short distance away but on the east coast and has a range of higher market range hotels such as Hyatt etc. We have the remaining two nights there which included a trip up to Ubud in the centre of the island which is popular in itself and offers really great scenery as an alternative to the beach scenes.

Finally, on 22nd we board a Qantas 767-300 but back to Sydney overnight, and following morning I ride on a BAe 146 of East West Airlines (a new type for me so see details below) back to Gold Coast airport.

Bae 146-300

The Bae (British Aerospace) aircraft 100 series first flew September 3rd, 1981 and entered service with Danair in May 1983. It was designed as a short haul regional airliner and was successful in filling this role. 387 were built so it became the best-selling British jet.

It is powered by four Lycoming bypass turbofan engines which gives it a whisper quiet performance and at one stage was the only jet allowed to land at London City airport. Initial series aircraft the 100 usually carried 70 in a five-abreast arrangement. Later the 200 and 300 were stretched versions and seating increased to around 94.

Bae originally produced this airplane and built in all 221 units, but as from 1992 AVRO started to build 166 of their model called an RJ (Regional Jet) which also included several other versions within that number of units but always preceded by the name AVRO. Towards the end the final three built were an improved version called the RJX but this never went into production.

VH-EWI was my first flight in a 146 and belonged to East-West airlines which later became absorbed into Ansett airlines. The plane was delivered to East West on August 25th, 1990 and my flight was Sydney to Gold Coast in Queensland on March 23rd, 1992. The plane then went to UK operators and was retired in March 2007.

I have flown 9 sectors on the 146, seven of them in Australia with East West or Qantas and two with Atlantic Airways on visit to the Faroe Islands in the north Atlantic (see May 2004).

Bae146-300 March 1992. On arrival Gold Coast.

April to Sydney

Down to Sydney for a wedding. Rachel, Bill and Joyce's granddaughter, is getting married!

So, we fly down on an East West BAe 146 on April 3rd, and we had two nights down there having a great time and returned on April 5th, on EWI the same aircraft I'd flown on only thirteen days earlier!

December to Melbourne/Snowy Mountains

We decided to have a break over Christmas and New Year. Our consultant Betty had left and gone back live in UK, but travel agency work is very quiet at that time, and with so many holiday days over that period we closed the agency and reopened early in the New Year. We travelled down Gold Coast to Melbourne on December 25th, on a TAA 737-300 and had five nights seeing the sights.

Had a day trip to Phillip Island to see fairy Penguins come ashore at dusk (Little Penguin is the correct name). Also, had a day trip out to the Dandenong ranges, part of it on the 'Puffing Billy' steam train and onto the Healesville Sanctuary which is another great day trip from Melbourne.

Also, caught up with Gordon who now worked for TAA, who had been one of the Prestwick crowd back in the early 1960s and briefly had been with me in BEA before coming out to Australia in the mid-1960s. After that we drove NE to Thredbo in the snowy Mountains and had four nights there.

Even in late December/early January, there was still snow on top of Mt Kosciuszko Australia's highest mountain which we climbed during our stay. We were joined by Anne's brother David who had taken up residence in Sydney in 1986. Finally, on January 3rd, we drove up from Thredbo to Sydney and flew up to Gold Coast on a TAA 737-300.

1993

No gadding about this year! At our village, our landlord was building a bigger shopping centre just adjacent to our present location, so Mudgeeraba was for the first time to have a supermarket plus an increase in other retail outlets. We were given the option to move from our present location and take up a tenure in the central courtyard of the new centre, and we were happy to make the move, giving us more exposure in what would be a busier area of the village.

So that occupied quite a lot of our time during the year preparing for and making the move.

1994

Once we had relocated, business started to increase and Betty was rehired as she had returned from UK after not successfully settling in back there. Also, we had another consultant Aaron who joined us fresh out of travel training academy. It was also around now that one of the discount airlines trying to compete with Qantas and Ansett on the domestic routes called Compass 2 (Compass 1 had already gone by the wayside) went into liquidation.

This brought about a big auction of their equipment including reservation consoles of which, I managed to acquire three at good price which were duly installed into our office onto the Sabre network. David, Anne's brother who is in IT came up from Sydney to do the connection work!

March to Vanuatu

Now I get to have a famil to Vanuatu. Departure is on March 4th from Brisbane to Port Vila on Air Vanuatu 737-400. This is a close neighbour of Australia so flight time is only 2hrs 19mins. We stayed two nights in overwater bungalows on Iririki Island only a short ferry trip away from the town.

We had the usual tour of several hotel properties but also did a circuit around the island and on the north coast saw filming locations used in the film "South Pacific".

On the 6th, we departed on same aircraft as the outbound flight named 'Spirit of Vanuatu', but had to call at Noumea, which turned out to be one of the more memorable landings I've been in! Just as we were touching down on a wet night, a cross wind gust from the right all but touched the left-wing tip onto the runway!

The crew saved the day but it was an unexpected gust just at the wrong moment. Then a 2hr 3mins sector from Noumea to Brisbane.

April

This was a really tough moment in my life to handle. My nephew, Paul, in UK was getting married on April 23rd. My brother from NZ and I were both planning to go, and in fact our flights would be the same plane from Singapore to LHR on April 19th.

On the week prior to that, I was feeling a bit under the weather, rather itchy and irritable and went to see my GP who was also a friend of mine. Still remember to this day the nice smile or smirk that came over his face when he proudly announced I had 'Chicken Pox'.

And me, just about to turn fifty-two years of age. Well, naturally UK plans got cancelled and I went home to bed and Tony, my doctor, came later to visit me at home and admitted it was the worst case of the disease he'd ever seen! Mentally I had to come to terms with not going to the wedding at such short notice which I found so hard to do.

May to Sydney to Join a Cruise

I got to the point where I was no longer contagious, and Anne and the crew at the agency sent me off on a Fairstar Cruise famil that had been offered.

I went down to Sydney on May 4th on a Qantas 737-400 (the series models are going up now) and had one night with Bill and Joyce, and then boarded Sitmars Fairstar Cruise ship the next afternoon for a departure out through Sydney heads in the evening dusk.

It was a nine-night cruise visiting Port Vila (Twice in two months for me), then to a Mystery isle, then to Noumea, our final stop before a few nights sailing back to Sydney. My first cruise ever but a very enjoyable experience and I think I needed it after my rather traumatic time.

Back into Sydney on the 14th May and a Qantas 737-400 brought me back up from Sydney to Gold Coast.

June to Cairns

Ansett gave us both the opportunity to have a three-night weekend trip to Cairns. That's about a two-hour flight north of Brisbane and well into the Tropics, so even in June very nice and warm.

We left on June 10th but with heavy Friday night traffic just made the flight with minutes to spare! The planes were 737-300 both ways. This was a first trip to Cairns for both of us and we stayed on an Esplanade hotel to the north of town. Walked around town first day, and following day went up to Kuranda on the Atherton Tablelands on the famed railway stopping at the Barron Falls enroute.

After having lunch up there, one option was to return on the cable car which gives you amazing views over the rainforest canopy and then reaching the edge of the escarpment a fantastic view of the Cairns coast, and out to the Coral sea as it lets down to the lower Cable station on the coastal plan. However, we were in only early 50s why not cycle back?

There was a company called Peregrine who organise such things including a 'sag' wagon if you want to give up pedalling but most of it (90%) was downhill, so both Anne and I made it! You will see from later in the book, we revisit the far north quite a few times. June 13th, we headed back south to Brisbane flight time 1hr 53mins.

October to NZ

UTAG were holding their AGM in Auckland so I headed off on October 13th, on an Air NZ 767-200 for two nights in Auckland. The AGM took up Thursday and Friday nights until Saturday lunchtime. I was able to delay my return flight and use my trip over to NZ to get down to visit my brother, but there was to be a bonus on this trip.

My brother's town in NZ was Hastings which is about 20 kms south of Napier. They are both in Hawke Bay (often called Hawke's Bay) and Hastings hosts each year a cycle race in October, called "Around the Bays". There are varying distances but my brother and I are, though keen, average cyclists; so entered the 55 km distance but other better cyclists go for longer distances.

Saturday PM I headed out from the city to Auckland airport and boarded a flight to Napier operated by an Air NZ SAAB 340 which is a new type for me (see details below). The SAAB 340 I think is an impressive feeder liner and is somewhat faster than the Friendship which was previously on this route. Flight time was 55mins compared with previous times of just over the one hour.

Saturday night was first night at my brothers, and then Sunday on a bike my bro loaned me, he and his youngest son, Mark, and myself, all rode the 55 kms in around 2hrs 20mins. Then I had the rest of the week at Stewart's (I have to give him his name sometimes) and came home on October 22nd, with SAAB 340 to Auckland, then a leased 747-200 from Malaysian Airlines operated by Air NZ crew over to Brisbane flight time 3hrs 3mins.

SAAB 340A

This popular twin engine turboprop regional airliner first flew January 25th, 1983. It could carry 33 passengers in a three-abreast seating and entered service with Swiss operator Crossair in June 1984. It's powered by 2 General Electric turboprop engines and 459 units have been produced.

ZK-NLR was first flown in Sweden by airline Swedair in August 1987 and joined Air Nelson in NZ on July 15th, 1994. My flight operated by Air NZ link was from Auckland to Napier (Hawkes Bay Airport) on October 15th, 1994. It remained in NZ for a number of years and went to the USA in 2007.

In all I've flown on eight Saab340 sectors four of them on the above route and four were with BA flight numbers operated by Logan Air on different sectors in Scotland in 2008.

SAAB340A October 1994. Prior to departure Auckland.

December to Japan

Ansett were now operating Internationally with two 747-300's to Hong Kong and the recently opened Kansai airport in Osaka Bay. They offered our agency two tickets to each working partner in the agency so we were able to travel as a family of three with Amy, and chose to go to Osaka.

This was to be over Christmas, so we departed Gold Coast to Sydney on an Ansett 737-300 on Christmas eve, and transferred over to the international terminal on an airside bus onto one of their 747-300's. Flight time going up from Sydney 8hrs 50mins.

The landing (if we can call it that) was surreal. The whole experience was like nothing I have felt before or after! I was not aware we had landed! Not a single bump! This aviator knew his stuff!

Then we taxied into the gate and Kansai as the airport is called, is a very futuristic style terminal, very high ceilings like a sci-fi interstellar space station. Then the announcements came across clear but in seemingly hushed tones as though a shuttle was arriving into gate 20 from galaxy nine. More to follow on this. The Capt had been Jones.

After a train ride to nearby Kyoto for a two night stay we saw the beautiful golden Kinkakuji temple just outside the city, we headed west for our next stay at Fukuoka for a two-night stay.

Sadly, despite me telling Anne the Shinkansen was very reliable and on time, the train in front broke down and we were stopped on the tracks for 45mins. Most unusual! From Fukuoka, we did a day trip down to Nagasaki to visit the Peace museum there. A beautiful town surrounded by hills.

Our visit had its drama with Amy collapsing in the peace museum (probably due to not having a proper breakfast) and we were all bundled into an ambulance, and spent several hours in a Roman Catholic funded hospital before Amy was discharged. The bill was a very nominal $70. Maybe we got taken there as they think foreigners can't pay the normal Japanese hospital costs but we had travel Insurance of course!

Following day, we headed east on the Bullet train all the way to Tokyo with minimal stops and I think the journey took about 6hrs for a distance just under 1100 kms!

We had three nights in Tokyo seeing the sights. Sadly, Anne was laid up some of the time with a bad back but Amy and I got out to see some sights. Later on, Anne and I went out to meet up with Margaret, a friend of mine, who had been a client through our travel agency. She lived and worked in Tokyo and was my go-between in helping me run a tour to Japan.

Amy had stayed in the hotel room for the evening so on our return from Margaret's place by train then taxi, the driver indicated in his broken English, there had been a quake. On returning to the room Amy said, "There's been a heck of a party going on upstairs, the whole rooms been shaking!"

We then told her the news! Finally, for our last night we headed west via Nagoya and spent New Year's Eve up in the Japanese alps at Takayama where I had been before with the Japan famil group. This time it was snowing! Anne and I had a walk around the town and surrounds in the falling snow.

Next morning, it was bright and clear and we headed back down via Nagoya to Kansai for the flight home. On the way down, the distance from the rail track we were on, looking east to Mt Fuji is a 140 kms and you could see it clearly in the distance, the air was so clear that winters day!

On New Year's Day night, we flew back on Ansett's sister ship to the one we had flown up on, this time straight into Brisbane with flight time 8hrs 9mins.

1995

On our return to work, I was talking with a client and mentioned we had been to Japan and how good the landing had been! He knew some of the Ansett crew and said he was putting money on that it was Capt. Jones, and sure enough when I checked my flight log when I got home he had been the Capt. on the flight!

A sequel to the Japan trip, was that in the Osaka area actually in Kobe, it was hit by a really severe earthquake of 6.9 on January 17th, only sixteen days after we had departed on our homeward journey from Kansai airport. Perhaps the quake in Tokyo had been the lead up to it.

May to Noumea

We made a decision to move from our house that we had been in since Christmas 1982.

It was taking too long to complete with limited time off from work, there was still no landscaping or garden to speak of and many other jobs needed doing in the limited time I had off. Anne found us a really good house in a suburban style block in the early months of the year in the village of Mudgeeraba, where our agency was located so just prior to the move we had a week's break in Noumea.

New Caledonia is Australia's nearest overseas neighbour, hence flight times are fairly short.

We departed Brisbane on a Qantas 737-400 on April 29th, and flight was only 1hr 46mins. One option which we sometimes do on a narrow body aircraft with single aisle is to have what is termed cross aisle seating. On say a 737 or an A320 the seating is 3-3 and the seats we would have allocated are the C and D seats and talk across the aisle. Try it sometime.

We stayed seven nights at Club Med. I learnt to sail a Laser yacht whilst I was there, but at the end in the short competition race, managed to get it totally overturned but did get it upright again and finished the course! Unfortunately,

Anne was sick towards the end of the stay, so we cancelled the hire car we planned to have, to do a bit of touring round the south end of the country.

The back end of town away from the waterfront is very much built in the French style of architecture. Overall it was a good break marred a little by Anne being unwell at the end. May 6th we boarded another Qantas 737-400 for the trip back to Brisbane. A few days later we had moved into our present house in Mudgeeraba.

September via Hong Kong to Macau

The UTAG AGM comes up this time of year and always to a new destination. This time to Macau at that time leased to the Portuguese but shortly to be handed back to China. Some of the SE Queensland agents including myself, left on September 7th, on a Qantas 767-300 via Cairns to Hong Kong.

The interesting thing about our departure from Brisbane is that the new international terminal had been duly opened two days prior, by Paul Keating, the Prime Minister at the time. New terminal was located about one mile to the east of the old terminal where our flight departed from. They were obviously in the process of what they now call a 'soft' opening.

On arrival into Kai Tak (always an exciting arrival seeing everyone's washing on the line!) as you make a sharp right hand turn to land, we were transferred in the harbour to a hydrofoil ferry that took us west over to Macau.

We stayed there for three nights for the AGM and one night they had a fireworks competition for four nations which really was outstanding! I had time to go down to the southern islands which are quieter and also reflect a lot of the Portuguese influence in the architecture and street signage and as Portugal is one of my favourite destinations, that was a worthwhile detour for me.

On the 10th, we returned by hydrofoil to Hong Kong and most were going back to Australia but I stayed two extra nights in Hong Kong, and following day headed up through the New Territory to the Chinese border. I had obtained a Visa to enter, but on the sketchy information I had, it gave me the impression the next city over the border Shenzhen was some 30 kms to the north.

After I'd cleared through immigration I came into a big long hall which I took to be the rail station where I would buy the necessary rail ticket. However, I couldn't make myself understood, so turned around went out through an exit door to the streets and found a towering skyline resembling MANHATTAN! Knock me down with a feather I was in Shenzhen! That was a big surprise!

After walking around some of the city including some parks, I came back to the border and returned into the New Territory of Hong Kong. On the way, back into Kowloon I stopped at a reserve with tall trees and walking trails and did some bird watching which is a hobby of mine. This is a side of some cities you don't get to see.

I got back into Kowloon for my final night and next day, September 12th, I flew out of Kai Tak airport on a Qantas 767-300 with flight time of 8hrs 33mins into Brisbane, this time arriving at the new terminal but it only has eight gates which are all full, so we watched "Vicar of Dibley" for 15mins waiting for a gate! I record landed time and then on the 'blocks' and the difference was 23mins!

November to Tasmania

Qantas Holidays invite me away on a famil to Tasmania. All the southern states of Australia have daylight saving time in the summer, so flights out of Queensland get scheduled early to make up for the hour we lose heading south so we leave at 5.10 AM! I haven't been up that early since my Panam days!

10 November, we head south from Brisbane to Melbourne on a 737-400 and connect onto 737-300's for the remainder, the next sector being to Hobart. We have one night in Hobart seeing many of the sights and as we had gone down on a Friday, Saturday AM we were able to visit the famed Salamanca markets which are a must, so make sure you include a Sat if you visit Hobart.

Saturday PM, we travelled west across Tasmania to Cradle Mountain and stayed at the lodge there that night. There are some great views close to the lodge over Dove lake with Cradle mountain beyond. Famils are all too short, a longer time would be nice but I do return later.

Sunday, we head along the north coast east towards Launceston for our last night which has many attractions to visit plus we saw some great places on the way. So, after Sunday night there, it was Monday, the 12th, and we departed Launceston via Melbourne to Brisbane.

1996

March to Sydney

This was a trip to Sydney to celebrate Bill and Joyce's fiftieth wedding anniversary. Joyce is my second cousin on my dad's side. Well, I can remember being at their wedding in 1946 and getting drunk at the tender age of four on the small amounts of beer left in the glasses at the reception bar in East London!

They emigrated out to Australia in the 1960s but we have also stayed in touch. My brother also came over from NZ for the event.

Anne and I flew down on March 8th on a Qantas 737-300 but this was in Solomons colours and named 'Guadalcanal', and would normally be used on the Honiara route.

We stayed down there for two nights enjoying the festivities and returned home on the 10th on a more normal Qantas 737-300. Photo below taken during the celebrations!

Bill and Joyce 50th Wedding anniversary Celebrations. Sydney March 1996.

May to Sydney

Sadly, my favourite uncle, an elder brother to my mother by two years, died on May 24th on his eighty-eighth birthday! At least aviation now allows us to move around with reasonable ease which was never the case many years ago, so I was able to be on a plane down the next day to Sydney to be with his daughter, my cousin, Evelyn, and his surviving wife, my aunt, Mary, and plane was a Qantas 737-400.

The funeral was on the 27th (which ironically happened to be my birthday of all dates) and I returned that evening on another Qantas 737-400.

A very sad weekend in our family.

September to Bangkok

Coming around to UTAG AGM time again and Bangkok is chosen for the venue.

The agents from the Brisbane area on September 19th board a Qantas 747-300 (my first ride on a Qantas one but they have been in the fleet for quite a long time now) and we fly non-stop to Bangkok flight time 8hrs 46mins. Overall I take four nights in Bangkok. With AGMs, there is the option to come straight home after the function which is usually a two-night stay but most agents especially if it's a first-time visit as mine was, will take the option of extra nights which I did.

The UTAG group arrange for day trips for those that stay on, and I took advantage of the trip out to the WW2 cemetery at Kanchanaburi and the Bridge over the river Kwai, and then a rail trip on some of the line that was constructed in WW2. A very moving and memorable day that I found worthwhile doing. Finally, after a bit of time to do shopping back in Bangkok, it was time to come home on September 23rd.

This time on a Qantas 767-300 but 2hrs 30mins late due awaiting connecting passengers. However, we made up over 30mins on the first sector to Cairns, then had what I can only describe as a 'blistering' turnaround at Cairns of 41mins. That's quick for a 767! Had they kicked all the tyres I wondered? but we travelled down to Brisbane at 41000ft and arrived only 45mins late!

October to NZ

Well, Stewart in NZ is telling me the "Round the Bays" cycle event is on again so I depart on an Air NZ 747-200 on October 6th, to Auckland and connect there onto a Saab 340 to Napier. I spend a week there with his family as the race is not until the following weekend. Sunday, 13th, we start off but I have been suffering from a cold so cannot give my best performance.

Again we do not break the two-hour barrier for the 55 kms ride which was our goal, but we enjoyed the event which was the main thing. Following day, I retraced my steps with a Saab 340 to Auckland and this time Air NZ operated a 767-300 back to Brisbane.

1997

March to NZ

Stewart reminds me there is also the 'Round lake Taupo' ride. This is by no means a race. Taupo is a large lake in the centre of the North island of NZ, so the ride starts at Taupo town situated at the northern end of the lake and it's a two-day weekend event starting on the Saturday going down the west side of the lake to a camp site that has been set up with tents for the cyclists to overnight in.

Then on the Sunday a return is made up the east side back into Taupo town. Anne came with me and we set off on Wednesday, March 12th, but didn't get on the morning flight (these things happen with our tickets), so we travelled over on the evening flight, which gave me a second ride on the Qantas 747SP that had taken me to Bali.

We had planned to stay with old Air NZ friends but too late for that, so stayed at an airport motel and saw them briefly next AM and headed to Tauranga, staying a night with Marnie. We missed seeing Ken. He had resumed flying and was now working for Air Pacific based in Fiji so was often away.

Next morning was the Friday so we headed off past Rotorua to arrive Taupo and meet up with Stewart and got into some accommodation for the night. I had taken a bike over with me from Brisbane and hired a station wagon at Auckland airport.

On Saturday, Anne followed us round Lake Taupo meeting up with us at breaks and lunch stops etc. and at south end of the lake, Stewart knew of someone with a weekender (called a Bach, pronounced batch), and we stayed in that rather than under the canvas the event people had provided. Just as well as it was actually a fairly cold wet night! Next day was a much easier day back into Taupo so we were relaxing in mineral spas by mid-afternoon.

North of the lake there is a thermal resort called DeBretts and where their thermal water spills out into the lake, there used to be little gravel pools in the last 20 m or so, where one or two people could enjoy a nice soak! That was back in 1969.

Well the water is still there of course, but things have changed a bit, and you are hard pressed to find a bit of a hollow to lay in, but for old times' sake, Stewart and I found one or two on Monday AM. Then I had to head back to Auckland visiting one of my old Panam loadmasters on the way (Brian who had joined on the same day as me). He was now working for an Aviation company in Hamilton, then dropped my car in Auckland and flew home to Brisbane on an Air NZ 767-300.

Anne stayed in NZ for a week and went back to Hastings to stay with Stewart and his wife, Brenda.

Future Thoughts

Anne and I had been in retail travel now for over thirteen years and felt we had reached a point where we wanted out, to maybe do something different. I was fifty-five years of age, so it was feasible if we were thoughtful about how we planned the future I could go into partial retirement. In any event, we put the agency on the market for sale and were starting to get offers from various travel organisations.

September to Singapore

This would be my last AGM and headed to Singapore from Gold Coast Airport, our local airport via Sydney. Went down on a Qantas Airbus A300 (a new type for me so see details below). After arrival Sydney connected onto a Qantas 747-400 to Singapore.

What made this AGM more memorable for me, I was able to catch up with Lorraine who had been a fellow loadmaster in Panam back in Auckland. She had married a Panam ground engineer based in Sydney and moved there and opened a travel agency, and had joined the same travel group. I had visited her at the travel agency in south Sydney but it was good to be able to catch up over a whole weekend!

Our arrival Singapore was on Thursday evening. The AGM formalities were completed by Friday afternoon and we were transferred to the port, where we boarded the Superstar Gemini cruise ship which cruised up the east Malaysian coast to Tioman Island. On the Saturday, we were moored off the Island probably about 800 m away which you could barely see due to the Indonesian bush fires, bringing up smoke from the south at the time.

David, a fellow agent, and myself hired bikes once we reached the island and cycled probably around 6 kms down to the airport. They had around a 600 m airstrip with the most colossal brand new control tower you have ever seen! Somebody in government obviously had funds to use up!

Overnight, we sailed back down to Singapore and on Sunday night, September 14th, came back non-stop into Brisbane on a Qantas 747-300 with flight time of 6hrs 38 mins.

Airbus A300B4-200

Airbus was originally going to be a consortium of UK, France and Germany but UK withdrew and France and Germany went on to produce the world's first twin jet wide body jet airliner.

It first flew on October 28th, 1972 and entered service with Air France around eighteen months later on May 23rd, 1974. It couldn't be considered a long-haul aircraft but it had a useful range of 4000 nmi. Several improved versions were built including stretched aircraft right up to a 600-series and a legacy of this type is that the cross section of the fuselage went on to be used into the A340 and the A330 both detailed later in the book. A total of 561 have been built.

VH-TAE was originally delivered to TAA who commenced flying with the type July 22nd, 1981. TAA was renamed to Australian Airlines in 1986 and then merged into Qantas in 1992.

To remove some possible confusion later, from 2002 to 2006 the name Australian Airlines came into use again for a low-cost outlet for Qantas using 767s painted in a tan Aboriginal colour scheme operating to some Asian ports from Australia (see my Cairns trips July and September 2003).

By September 11th, 1997, when I flew on this A300 it was in Qantas colours on a QF flight number from Gold Coast Airport to Sydney. Flight time 1hr 10mins.

In December 1998, this plane was delivered to Pace Airlines as a freighter and has continued with other cargo operators since.

Photo below is TAE again thanks to Rob Finlayson

There are three complete A300s on display in the world in museums in Germany, South Korea and France.

Airbus A300B4-200 September 1997. Photo provided courtesy of Rob Finlayson.

October, A Big Day

Well the day has come when we can hand over the keys to new owners to the agency.

An experienced consultant from a nearby competitor travel group funded by her parents bought us out. My attention to detail I think had always helped me achieve what our repeat clients told us no other agent had ever done for them. We had never advertised. All our increase in business had purely come from satisfied customers spreading the word.

We now had a little time to take stock of our future. I was thinking that with all of the contacts I had made through the UTAG travel group that I could consider working part time at other agencies located on the Gold Coast. In between times, we still had some credits to use up in terms of travel so the next trip came into that category.

November to Canberra

Some of you may be aware of recumbent bikes but I have been riding them from the early 1990s. Nearly all of them home built. This is where the rider is lying down and the pedals are right up front. Many are two wheelers but quite a lot are trikes.

I have both but the trike I now ride exclusively, I've owned for around twenty-five years (see photo). Only as recent as 2020, perhaps to compensate for my advancing years, it now has an electric motor which allows me to ride it even in the midday summer heat (and it now has an overhead canopy).

Anyway, in November 1997 the Recumbent riders (Bent for short) have an annual rally and it was in Canberra.

The two-wheeler I had at the time was packed up and Anne and I flew down on a Qantas Bae146 Brisbane-Canberra on November 6th. Anne's friend had a Great aunt living there so we had four nights at her house, and I cycled out each day to the "Bent" rally which was out close to Canberra airport.

I didn't win any prizes but my two-wheeler does perform quite well. It's the rider that needs more power! It's not all about recumbents. I did get to ride a Penny Farthing during the weekend!

10 November, saw us coming back to Brisbane on the same 146 that took us down.

This is my Trike recumbent. I possessed it in 1997 but I took a 2 wheeler to Canberra for the event.

December

Leading up to Christmas, Japan Airlines asked me to work for them in the Surfers Paradise office for two weeks to help out whilst some staff were on leave.

1998

Into the New Year, Dallas who ran several UTAG agencies down on the Queensland/NSW border about 25 kms south, wanted a consultant to work Thursday evening, and Friday and Saturday. So I started to work down there, and that work lasted until mid-year 2000.

Also, further into the year another friend of mine Graeme who ran an agency up at the top end of the coast wanted some extra help on two days per week with start time 10 AM and finish at 5 PM on Monday and Tuesday. So, in the end over roughly most of 1998 and 1999, I ended up working around four and a half days per week. So much for a semi-retirement!

1999

February to Tasmania

We had arranged to join up with Bill and Joyce on a fly drive trip to Tasmania for eleven nights.

Anne and I flew down to Sydney on a Qantas 767-300 on February 10th to meet up with B and J and carry onto Launceston in a Qantas Bae146. We picked up a hire car and stayed on the east coast one night, then visited Port Arthur which was a convict prison in the 1800s. It's located to the east of Hobart.

We got to stay in Hobart, seeing Salamanca markets on a Saturday morning and while the others are driving around, I hired a bike and climbed Mt Wellington. At 1271 m high, that's not bad for a mediocre cyclist getting near to fifty-seven years!

Next, we head west to Cradle mountain and Strahan. At Strahan, we go on the Franklin river cruise across Macquarie harbour but by afternoon the wind coming from the NW has carved the harbour up into 12-foot-high waves, which catamarans do not like. Another one of my nasty cat rides. One more to come!

Then we drove along the north coast to Launceston, stopping to see the lovely murals on the sides of buildings in Sheffield. Whilst in Launceston for the last few nights Anne drove B and J around, and I hired a cycle and went out to nearby Evandale which was holding its annual Penny farthing rally!

Finally, we leave Launceston on February 21st, on a Qantas Bae146 to Sydney where we farewell B and J and Anne and I continue up to Gold Coast on a Qantas 737-300.

July to Scandinavia

This is a Pearler! Hang onto your hats. A leading tour wholesaler for Scandinavia ran an annual travel agent competition with first prize, a trip visiting all the capital cities and five nights cruising south on the Hurtigruten, the famed Norwegian Coastal voyage. Well yours truly won it!

31 July I departed Brisbane on a Thai airways (new airline for me) 747-400 via Sydney to Bangkok. There I connect onto a SAS 767-300 overnight to Copenhagen. I have two nights there visiting Tivoli Gardens and numerous other sights in the city plus next day up to Helsingor about 30 kms north of the city where the magnificent Kronborg castle, was the setting for "Hamlet".

Following morning, August 3rd, I'm on a SAS MD80 (McDonnell Douglas) a new type, see details below, enroute to Helsinki. I'd asked for a low-fat meal and duly got delivered to my seat a box which contained a banana!

Helsinki is a lovely city and aside from its normal Cathedral which stands head and shoulders in the city above everything else, also has Uspenski cathedral a Russian Orthodox church which is a must to visit. Any city with trams in it also gets my vote!

Night of August 4th, I leave Helsinki on Viking lines Ship MS Mariella west towards Stockholm arriving through the scattering of islands to the east of the city into Stockholm. I had two enjoyable days in Stockholm and visited Gamla Stan the old city. Also, went out to Bromma airport west of the city which has regional flights often with Bae146 aircraft.

The terminal was still 'old school' with swing doors! Nothing wrong with that in my book. I also had dinner with a friend of mine's son and his wife who lived there. Oddly enough, my friend in Australia lived in Sydney goes by the name Graham Hyslop (exactly the same as mine).

Our great-great-grandfathers were born in the same area of SW Scotland in the 1800s, although, we have never established a link, but the profile of our faces are uncannily similar. Strangely enough, Karl, his son, in Stockholm was doing contract work for SAS on the Sabre system. It really is a small world sometimes.

After my stay there, I flew onto Oslo on August 7th, on another SAS MD80. The Fornebu airport has now been closed and flights now go into Gardermoen about 40 kms to the north of Oslo, but the transfers are fast whether by bus or train, and it isn't long before one is in the city. I only had the one night there but managed to take a ferry over to see the museums which included the Kon Tiki raft and a preserved Viking long ship.

Sunday, August 8th, I was due to fly up to Kirkenes in northern Norway to connect onto the Hurtigruten cruise, but I asked the tour wholesaler as my flight was going via Tromso, could I break the journey there and make my own side trip up to Spitzbergen. I've been hankering to get there for years! If you get your Atlas out, you'll find it halfway from top end of Norway heading towards the north pole.

They said yes, so first sector was a SAS MD80 to Tromso then I transferred onto a Braathens 737-400 from there to Longyearbyen which is the town in Spitzbergen (or Svalbard is another name it is known by). Prior to landing the cabin announcements tell you not to leave town without a rifle in case you chance on a Polar bear! I don't think that happens many places!

Midnight Sun at Longyearbyen airport midnight on August 9th. Sun doesn't dip below horizon until August 22nd.

I had four nights there. First full day was the 9th (Anne's birthday story to come) so I headed off on a boat trip to Barentsberg which is further down the Fjord. The Russians mine for coal here and we arrived around noon, and Anna, our tour guide on our boat for the day, handed us over to a Russian tour guide named Olga in Barentsberg for the shore excursion.

We had to be back on board by 2 PM so I stayed with the group until 1 PM and was getting the talk from Olga in a very heavy Russian accent telling how many people were mining, how many wives were here etc.

Well, at 1 PM, the tour carried on and I stayed in the hotel by the phone, used my Norwegian phone card to call Anne at home and wish her a happy birthday and have a talk. After that, I made my own way back through the buildings towards the boat taking my time and got to the boat at 1.55. Everyone else was on board down below having lunch.

Anna suggested I joined them but as we were just about to cast off I stayed on deck but around the corner of the wheelhouse out of the rather stiff breeze, and then heard Olga call out to Anna in absolutely plain English, "OK, Anna, see you Friday!" I poked my head around the corner of the wheelhouse and that was the moment when she had been rumbled!

Well later that evening, I borrowed a bike and cycled the few kms out to the airport which had good view to the north, and took the photo which you can see on the previous page of the midnight sun! The sun is 24hrs a day until August 22nd, then by September 22nd, it's the equinox: 12hrs of sun 12hrs of night. Then by October 22nd, the sun disappears for 4 months until February 22nd! I was just 705 nmi from the North pole.

Another day with a guide I did a plateau hike above the town. This was where one of two Swiss girls without a guide and without a rifle was attacked by a bear and was killed.

What you need out of town in Svalbard. A 303-rifle strapped to your crossbar In event, you chance on a Polar Bear!

And on another I hired a bike to travel out of town but you can't go out of town without packing so to speak! In case you meet a Polar bear, you have to take a rifle, so I took a 303 duly strapped to the handle bars (see photo). It's one way of getting the cars to give you a wide berth!

On the way, I went past the airport and I think it might be the only place in the world (at least it was then) when you would go into the terminal with the rifle slung over your shoulder and not leave it unattended outside! On this day, I cycled further out of town to bear valley (didn't see one) but did see a Svalbard Reindeer pictured below.

Svalbard Reindeer on a cycling trip outside the town of Longyearbyen. August 1999.

That brings us to the end of the Spitzbergen stay.

Next day, August 12th, I depart on another Braathens 737 this time a 700-series to Tromso a lovely city for a one night stay.

Next day, I resumed my SAS journey leaving Tromso on an MD80 via Alta to land in Kirkenes.

I had the afternoon free, so hired a bike and cycle out as far as the Russian border about 12 miles out of town then back to the hotel for the evening.

Next day, folks staying at the hotel joining the southbound Hurtigruten cruise are transferred out to the wharf about one mile out of town. We leave on the MV Nordlys which is one of the newest in the fleet built in 1994. They are working ferries but they do have cruise ship like cabins, dining rooms, fitness gym and lookout lounges etc.

The cruise has daily sailings from Bergen and takes six nights going north to Kirkenes and then five on the southbound return going south. There are 40 ports to call at, but the schedule is mainly designed that those doing the round trip will see all the ports in daylight. Those they miss at night going north they will generally visit during the day going south.

Often there are excursions where passengers can leave the ship at one port and join later at a point further along on the voyage. I did this in the Lofoten Islands and did get back there in 2019 to see more of this enchanting area. Also at the time, there were two smaller ships in the fleet which were called Traditional and only carried 140 passengers and really looked the part of an old style small liner.

Well later on the 2019 trip I managed to sail on the one remaining traditional aptly named MV Lofoten.

After a really enjoyable cruise south to Bergen, arrived there on August 19th, and had some time to visit some spots I'd become familiar with back in 1968.

Following morning, August 20th, left Bergen on Air UK Fokker F50 (a new type so see details below) and arrived Aberdeen 1hr 23mins later.

My brother was there to meet me and we picked up a hire car and drove west to stay one night at Fort William. This is nestled under Ben Nevis the highest mountain in the UK which we climbed in bright sunny weather the next day. Had lunch at the top complete with the strains of a bagpipe playing!

After descending, we had time left in the day with the long daylight hours at that time of the year to start heading south and spent an overnight on the journey.

Next day, we arrived south of Edinburgh to Melrose, where we stayed and walked the Eildon hills which is a place our father had spent time as a young boy.

The rest of time with Stewart was spent travelling further south visiting friends and relatives until finally I leave from my sister's place NW of London on September 4th for the journey home.

Firstly, a SAS MD80 from LHR to Copenhagen connecting onto a SAS 767-300 overnight to Bangkok flight time 10hrs 41mins. Sadly, the only film I had left in my camera over exposed the good views of the Himalaya range out of the left-hand side of the plane, but two attempts later in 2019, I eventually captured some decent images!

I stayed one night at Bangkok, relaxing near the airport (Don Mueang at that time) at a hotel complete with pool and return in evening of the 6th for my homeward flight. Departed Bangkok on Thai 747-400 to Sydney then up to Brisbane, arriving September 7th.

One of the best trips of all time!

McDonnell Douglas MD80

This airliner was developed from the earlier DC9 and the Douglas company had been absorbed to become McDonnell Douglas by the time this aircraft was built. It was extended by over 14ft compared to the DC9-50 series and had a larger wing and carried 155 in a coach configuration on a range of up to 2600 nmi.

It first flew on October 18th, 1979, and first service with Swissair was October 1980. Production ended in 1999 by which time, 1191 units had been built. It was not as fuel efficient as the 737 or the A320 which have continued in sales into the twenty-first century.

LN-RMA a Norwegian registered MD81 owned by SAS was first delivered to them on July 7th, 1987. My sector was from Copenhagen to Helsinki on August 3rd, 1999 with a flight time of 1hr 13mins.

It continued with SAS until 2004 when it was sold to a US operator and then was converted to an 83 series which had higher weights, more range with increased fuel tanks etc.

In all I have flown on seven MD80 sectors, six with SAS in Scandinavia and one in South America with Austral airlines. The photo shows a sister ship LN-RMD which flew me Tromso-Alta-Kirkenes some ten days later, all points up in the arctic circle.

In viewable museums, there are at least three MD80's in Puerto Rico, USA and Italy. In addition, there are planes but in Colleges and Technology Centres and the like which may need an appointment to view.

McDonnell Douglas MD80 August 1999. LN-RMD is a sister ship flown on ten days later Tromso-Alta-Kirkenes.

Fokker F50

As Fokker Friendship F27 sales started to slow down, it was decided to bring out an updated version to be named the Fokker F50. It was to be powered by two Pratt and Whitney turboprops of 2250 shp each, instead of the original Dart engines and seating capacity was 62 seats with range of 1100 nmi and cruise speed of 286 kts.

First flight was on December 28th, 1985 and entered service in 1987. 213 of this new model were built and it achieved 30% fuel reduction compared with the previous F27.

G-UKTI the plane I flew on had its first flight in April 1995 and moved to KLM in January 1998.

My flight on August 20th, 1999 was from Bergen to Aberdeen, and although, basically in KLM colours was an operation by AIR UK with an Air UK flight number. Photo kindly provided by David Oates of sister ship, G-UKTD.

Aircraft was later ferried to Maastricht in 2010, then to Indonesia where it was registered as PK-ECF. I've flown a total of three F50 sectors with the other two being domestic sectors in Iceland in May 2004.

Sadly, the Fokker company after a very long existence was struggling to remain profitable especially with the F50 and their other products when other options on the market such as the Saab340, ATR and Dash 8 were available and the company went into liquidation in 1997.

Fokker F50 August 1999. Shown is G-UKTD courtesy of David Oates

2000

September to Sydney for the Olympics

We had been planning to go down for a week leaving on the 20th. I had now started to work more hours for one agent on an area just behind Surfers Paradise called Isle of Capri, and the UTAG name had been changed to the Travelscene group. However, my boss, David, had sustained an ankle injury playing soccer ten days previously, oddly enough with a whole load of doctors and not one had realised he had snapped his Achilles tendon!

So fortunately, we were not due to see any Olympic events for the first few days of our stay, so whilst David had his op, I stayed two days in the office. Qantas kindly changed our tickets at no charge and we went down on September 22nd, a 737-300 down and a five-night stay with Bill and Joyce. We saw badminton in one session and some athletics in the main stadium.

We were also a few of the many assembled at Circular Quay watching Cathy Freeman Win Gold in the 400 m on a huge screen that had been erected there! I think it was rated a very successful games. On September 27th, we returned home on a Qantas 767-200 to Gold Coast.

Sadly, although Joyce had seemed fine when we were there in the September, shortly after that she was diagnosed with terminal cancer. Anne went down prior to Christmas to help out for several weeks, and we did see Bill and Joyce when they came up to the Sunshine coast early in the New Year. Sunshine Coast is located about 90 kms north of Brisbane whereas we are about 90 to the south.

2001

June to Sydney

Sadly, Joyce passed away in early June, so Anne and I travelled down to attend her funeral.

We departed Gold Coast Airport on June 6th, and returned on June 10th both on Qantas 737-300's. Joyce was a wonderful lady and has been sorely missed by all her family.

2002

February to NZ

We were invited to our nephew, Mark's wedding in Christchurch in NZ. Only reasonable way cost wise of getting there was to go via Wellington at the lower end of the North Island and take a flight over to Blenheim at the top end of the South Island next day. This then, gave us the chance to see parts of that area we had not seen before on our way down to the wedding.

We travelled over from Brisbane on an Air NZ 737-300 January 23rd, and overnighted Wellington noting that Queen Elizabeth 2nd was visiting NZ at the time on a trip to mark her 50th Diamond Jubilee and a BA 767 was parked on the apron as we landed.

Next day was another type for me on an Embraer Bandeirante 110, please see details below. Flight was from Wellington to Blenheim a distance of 51 miles and flight time of 19mins. The photo pages show the Bandeirante on arrival Blenheim.

Our journey concluded after the tying of the knot and various festivities in Christchurch by travelling on Air NZ 737-300's back from Christchurch through Wellington to Brisbane on 4th March.

Embraer Bandeirante 110

This Bandeirante was delivered to Skywest in Australia January 1992 and came to EAGLE AIR in NZ as ZK-VJG on April 28th, 2000. It subsequently returned to operating in Australia in March 2003 and is still listed as flying.

The type was first flown October 26th, 1968 in Brazil and initially built for the military. Passenger model first flew August 9th, 1972 and started service with Trans Brazil in April 1973. 15 to 21 passengers are carried. Production was stopped in 1990 after 494 had been produced. The Embraer Brasilia superseded this model.

Embraer Bandeirante 110 February 2002. On arrival Blenheim NZ.

2003

July to Cairns

We head up to Cairns for a seven-night holiday. This is a time when the Australian airlines name has been reintroduced, this time for a low-cost arm of Qantas using 767's in a tan Aboriginal colour scheme on oversea routes. On one route, they operate out of Gold Coast heading to Cairns before going on overseas.

We took advantage of this sector and travelled on their 767-300 on July 19th to arrive in Cairns. We had a car from the airport and drove to one of the beaches just to the north called Yorkey's Knob. From there other than relaxing on some days, we had a day trip visiting Daintree river, viewing Crocs there, Mossman gorge, and onwards to Cape Tribulation.

One thing I should mention about the drive north from Cairns to Port Douglas (PD) is once you are beyond Palm Cove and about half way to PD, you pass through a small hamlet called Ellis Beach, which just looks tropical. You could be anywhere!

It looks delightful and it makes you wonder why people spend lots of money rushing around various destinations when they have such places on their doorstep. Well I have proved the point because I've been back there twice since! The day to Cape Tribulation was a very full day but very worthwhile.

On another day, we drove over on the coastal plain to one of the stations on the Kuranda Railway to get picked up there, and rode up on the train to Kuranda, a repeat of what we had done on the earlier Ansett weekend, but this time came back on the Sky rail which gave great views over the Rainforest Canopy, and then letting down to the coastal plain, fantastic views of Cairns and the coral sea beyond. A really great week away.

The Australian flight back involves a very early flight (we aren't good at those) so we came back on July 26th on a Qantas 737-800 Cairns to Brisbane.

September to Cairns (Again)

This time Travelscene were having a three-night workshop in Cairns, so David at the Isle of Capri agency who I was working for virtually full time at this stage asked me to attend on behalf of the agency, which I was happy to do. On September 5th travelled up from Gold Coast airport to Cairns again on an Australian Airlines 767-300 but a different machine to the previous journey in July.

My travelling companion on the flight was the David I had been cycling with on Tioman island in Malaysia! We stayed at a centrally located hotel and there were a mixture of activities during the weekend. Flight home, again because Australian come through so early in the morning, was a later flight flying to Brisbane on September 8th on a Qantas 767-200.

September to Singapore

Later in the same month, Singapore Holidays, a wholly owned tour wholesaler branch run by Singapore airlines, offered me a place on a famil to Singapore. This was in the aftermath of the SARS epidemic and the uptake of sales by the public had been rather slow, so this famil was to encourage agents to help sell Asian destinations again.

Departure from Brisbane was on September 24th and was on an SQ 777-200, so a new type for me, so please see details below. It was an interesting time there. Yes, there were some hotel visits but some good points of interest were visited and a good lecture on the art of tea drinking. Vincent, the tea master, had a knack of captivating his audience! After three nights, there we came back on an overnight flight on September 27th, on another 777-200, flight time 6hrs 45mins.

Boeing 777-200

Boeing designed and built this large twin wide body jet to fill a gap between their 747 and the smaller 767. It has been a great success and to June 2021, 1667 planes have been built. It first flew June 12th, 1994 and entered service with United just under a year later on June 7th, 1995.

A stretched 300-series has been produced and extended range versions also. The 200 carries from 301 to 368 in three classes.

This SQ aircraft 9V-SRH was delivered to them in May 2001 and my flight was Brisbane to Singapore on September 24th, 2003.

It was moved to a Thai operator in 2015 and now stored at Alice Springs as at 2020.

I have flown on eight 777 sectors, six have been on SQ, one with Air NZ and one with Thai Airways.

Boeing 777-200 September 2003. 9V-SRM is a sister ship, courtesy of Rob Finlayson.

2004

January to Melbourne

Anne used to play tennis and is still an avid watcher of the sport on TV, so on this occasion we decided to go down to Melbourne to see some matches at the Melbourne open.

We travelled down on Virgin on January 21st, on a 737-800 and initially stayed the first four nights there taking in several tennis matches, seeing the likes of Lleyton Hewitt v Nadal, but there were many other names familiar to the scene at the time. On Monday, 26th, we headed west along the Great Ocean Road and stayed three nights at Apollo Bay, and on one day went further west to see the Twelve Apostles and other great creations down along the coast sculpted by nature. Finally, we headed back on the 28th towards Melbourne to have lunch with my friend Gordon (from my BEA days) and his wife. He had come out from UK and worked for TAA but was now retired.

We enjoyed the lunch and the afternoon and I got ourselves ready to go in the firm belief our flight was at 6 PM (as was the flight coming south). I was looking up my flight details when Gordon said in his very thick Glaswegian accent, "What's the flight number."

Just at that point I saw my itinerary and realised the flight left in 15mins at 4.30 PM! We said hurried goodbyes. Fortunately, they live only a mile from the terminal and we managed to drop the car and got to the check-in desk by 4.29 PM!

In Virgin rules, arriving one minute prior to STA allows you to rebook and only be charged if the new seats are higher in cost. However, while rebooking they found our scheduled flight hadn't even arrived into Melbourne so we were put back onto it and left at 5.15 PM! Even the old timers make mistakes now and again! Flight home was again on a 737-800.

May to Iceland

I'd planned the previous year to do a cycling trip around Iceland! This would have been on my recumbent bike which I have already mentioned in the 1997 trip to Canberra, but Iceland would have been on my trusty trike, but in the lead up rides my right Achilles tendon started to play up (and still does) so the trip got cancelled.

Then early in 2004, invitations went out to agencies to attend an Icelandic workshop to be held in Reykjavik in early May. I submitted an application on behalf of our agency which was approved so was given a place to attend.

I departed on a late-night flight May 7th from Brisbane on an SQ 777-200 and transferred in Singapore next morning onto a 747-400 to London, flight time 12hrs 45mins.

Stayed one night with Ron (my old BEA friend) and on May 9th departed LHR on an Icelandair 757-200 to Keflavik (a new type so see details below). Keflavik is the main international airport and is around 50 kms SW of the city.

The first 3 nights were spent in Reykjavík, the first full day being the workshop and the second they took us on a tour which is known as the "Golden Circle" which visits the original Geysir (after which all others are named), Gullfoss (translates to the Golden Falls), and Thingvellir which was the original seat of the Icelandic parliament set in the rift valley area between the American and European tectonic plates.

On the 12th May, we headed north out of the town airport on an Air Iceland Fokker 50 to Akureyi. This is on a Fjord on the north coast of Iceland. After being shown some of the sights of the town, we headed east towards our one night stay at the southern end of Lake Myvatyn. This area is inundated with areas of thermal activity. It's hard to take a photo without seeing steam coming out of the ground somewhere in the photo!

Next morning, we head back on an unsealed road NW towards a town on the north coast named Husavik. I would have cycled this the previous year! This terrain we travelled over literally looks like a moonscape and this is where the lunar astronauts trained. After a brief whale watch cruise at Husavik (no whales sighted unfortunately), we continued west back to Akureyi for the same Air Iceland Fokker 50 flight back to Reykjavík.

Next day, the 14th, after some morning sightseeing I caught a bus travelling east along the south coast to Hofn in SE Iceland. I have booked three nights here and hope to do a number of activities. Next day, I do get to travel with two others to a small island off the south coast where we see plenty of bird life, including I get up close and personal with Puffins for the first time.

Sadly, second day there are not enough numbers to do a Skidoo (Snowmobile is the other name for this transport) ride on VatnaJokull glacier, but my host at the accommodation kindly takes me up there which is an impressive 4WD trip and I get to see where the Skidoos operate from and get to sit on one for a photo!

17 May, I now leave Hofn flying westbound back to Reykjavík town airport. This time Islands Flug kindly provide me a seat and this is a Dornier 228, and again a new type, so see details below for this. Flight climbs right over Vatnajokull and I see below me the hut where I stopped at with the Skidoos the previous day! That gave me the rest of the day in Reykjavík until I fly out in the evening.

Atlantic Airways (based in the Faroes) used Bae146's at the time so can operate out of the town airport. I depart in the evening on a 200-series aircraft and flight time to the Faroes is 1hr 15mins.

I stay three nights in the Faroes guest of their inbound tourism department and they show me around on both of the full days. The travel photo shows a grass roofed dwelling out of town but many in the town are also roofed the same way.

Typical of the houses in the Faroe Islands even in town. This is on the west cost of the main island of Stremoy.

20 May, I fly out of the Faroes towards Aberdeen on the same 146 and the same crew and flight time just 58mins.

My brother met me at the airport (that seems to be our regular meeting point), and over the next nine nights we work our way down the UK visiting the usual friends and relatives.

Finally, on May 29th, I depart LHR on a midday SQ 747-400, flight time 12hrs 9mins, to Singapore then an SQ 777-200 on 30th to Brisbane with a very fast time of 6hrs 26mins. Again, I think this is in the top four of my fastest flights. A good Jetstream pushed us along to cover the 3818 miles an average speed between the two cities of 593 mph!

A brilliant trip!

Boeing 757-200

This narrow body twin jet was designed as a successor to the 727 and still uses the same cross section fuselage the same as from the 707. The type first flew February 19th, 1982, and entered service just under eleven months later on January 1st, 1983 with Eastern Airlines. It could carry 200 passengers in two classes over a range of 3900 nmi.

A 23ft stretched 300-series introduced in September 1996, seated 243 over a similar distance. Overall, 1050 of this aircraft were built.

TF-FIO was delivered to Icelandair in April 1999 and operated my flight LHR to Keflavik on May 9th, 2004. At time of writing, this plane is still in the airline's fleet. Photo shows FIO on arrival at Keflavik.

One 757-200 is on display in Delta colours in their museum in Atlanta USA.

Boeing 757-200 May 2004. On arrival Keflavik.

Dornier 228

This aircraft developed by the Dornier company from their previous 28 model, is a STOL machine capable of operating into unpaved strips, and short runways which other more conventional planes are not suited for. Its first flight was on March 28th, 1981 and entered service July 1982.

It carried 17 passengers with a two-pilot crew and is powered by two Garrett AiResearch turboprop engines. Germany has built 245 and 125 have been licence built in India.

TF-ELF shown in the photo was first delivered to Norway in January 1985 and first registered in Iceland June 1993. My flight from Hofn (SE Iceland) west to Reykjavik on May 17th, 2004 flew over the glacier Vatnajokull which is the highest ice cap in the country, and is just under 7000ft high and occupies close to 8% of Iceland's land area. The ice cap is shown in the background in the photo.

This plane was still flying in the UK as at 2015.

Dornier 228 May 2004. Prior to departure Hofn. Vatnajokull glacier shows in background.

October to Sydney

Anne and her friend, Jan, went down to Sydney to stay in the Blue mountains about an hour and a half's drive west of Sydney They left on October 23rd, and hired a car on arrival down there. I followed on the 29th, on a Virgin 737-800 and took a train out to the Blue mountains to join up with them for one night.

On the 30th, we came back into Sydney and saw Jan, off north on a flight to Queensland, and we spent the next three nights around the area where Bill still lived, catching up with his family and also meeting Stewart, my brother, from NZ who was also there.

So, it was a good family time. We returned to the Gold Coast on November 2nd, this time on a 737-700 of Virgin.

2005

A Decision Time

By this time, my hours with David at Isle of Capri had slowly increased, to the point I was now working full time and the workload I was handling was quite enormous. I spoke with David and it was decided that as I had a holiday coming up in May, this would be a good point to scale back to two or three days on my return so that is in fact what was agreed.

May to Canada/Alaska

Anne had always wanted to see Canada so we departed Brisbane on Air NZ on a 747-400 on May 17th, connecting in Auckland onto the same type to LA and flight time on that second sector was 11hrs 05mins. This would be one of my fastest sectors covering the 6522 miles between the two cities in that time, comes out at an average speed of 588 mph! We connected in LA onto an Alaska Airlines 737-700 to Seattle.

We had two nights there, and on the full day we had a hire car and made the trip up to see the Boeing plant north of Seattle at Everett, which was really great. Then by ferry we headed from Seattle to Victoria on Vancouver Island, and enjoyed our time there before taking transfer by bus and ferry over to Vancouver where we saw all the major sights during our three nights there.

After that we picked up a hire car, stopping at Whistler, the ski resort, for a short while and staying the night at Kamloops, before arriving at Banff for two nights. Anne had a cousin in Calgary so we made a daytrip to visit them and had a really enjoyable time but had only just got back on the highway heading west back to Banff, when our car slowly came to a halt at 10 PM at night! This is embarrassing!

I've been a flight planning officer and I've run out of fuel! My only defence is that the dashboard is not designed for somebody of my height, so the fuel warning indicator was out of sight behind the bars of the steering wheel. It was then I thought back and realised, the last fuel we had put in was way back in Kamloops!

Fortunately, a First Nation native in a very old van (full of kids) stopped and offered to get fuel, but then as well as needing the money for that, said he would need money to fill up himself! So, he headed off with $40 of our money. Yes, he did turn up an hour later still with all the kids in the van. They all thought it was very exciting!

Next day, leaving Banff I could show Anne Lake Louise which still had ice at one end of the lake and then we headed north up through the Columbian Icefield Highway, stopping at Lake Peyto to show how carefully Anne had coordinated her wardrobe attire (see photo), then past the Athabasca glacier which I had been as far as, on my previous visit in 1966. This time we kept going north and spent two nights in Jasper.

Then on my birthday, drove west past Mt Robson which at nearly 13,000ft. is the highest point in the Canadian Rockies. We saw two separate sightings of Black bears this day as we were driving. Having arrived at Prince George our destination for the night, I dropped off the car at the airport, and next morning we caught Canadian Rail from there on a full day's journey west to Prince Rupert for a two-night stay.

This was a great place to visit with Bald Eagles right in town giving aerial displays. However, on the morning we were due to leave, it was to be on the Alaska Marine highway which is the ferry system that serves all the west coast of Alaska. Our departure was due at 10 AM but I rang at 8.30 and found it was cancelled and a replacement was being offered at 5 PM that night.

We had to go down to the ferry terminal to get new confirmed tickets to Ketchikan, but then rest of the day was free. In hindsight, (why is that always 20/20?) I should have canvassed other travellers and seen if we could have all chartered a De Havilland Beaver and flown up there during the day! As it was we missed our flight out of Ketchikan which the on-time boat would have connected us onto.

This meant we missed our first of two nights in Juneau and a day trip up Fjords the next day. So got to Ketchikan gone midnight had the most expensive (and sub-standard) hotel of the whole trip, then got to Juneau the next evening, 24hrs late on an Alaskan 737-400.

After a night Juneau, we were back on schedule, had a little time to see the town (the capital of Alaska) and on the way to pick up our next ferry sector, the taxi had time to take us to visit the Mendenhall Glacier on the way to the wharf. The ferry took us via way of Haines for a stay and then to Skagway. Then we travelled on the White Pass and Yukon railway from Skagway.

Even in early June, there was lots of ice and snow and it was pretty cool when we got to the end of the line and changed over to a bus to take us on into Whitehorse in the Yukon.

Lake Peyto in the Canadian Rockies. Annie paying careful attention to be colour coordinated! May 2005.

After the night, we were heading to Fairbanks but I had a treat in store for Anne! On June 5th, we travelled on Air North on their Avro 748 service which had two stops enroute (this is a new type for me so details are below); the second stop giving Anne a landing well inside the Arctic circle! Old Crow relies on its air connection. There is no other transport into this place, only the plane!

The day we visited, it was a sunny day and a balmy 20° C but come December, when the sun isn't even above the horizon that would be another story! Here I will briefly explain an image included below.

On the sector from Old Crow to Fairbanks just short of halfway, from the right hand of the plane you will see the meandering of one of the many tributaries of the Yukon River. In doing this, occasionally segments of the river get silted up and get 'left behind' and these are called oxbow lakes. This photo is one of the best examples I've seen.

We had several nights in Fairbanks and with hire car visited Denali National Park heading south to Anchorage, and then finally had nights down at Seward and had a day cruise out of Whittier seeing the many glaciers in Prince William Sound.

Oxbow Lakes. Enroute from Old Crow Yukon to Fairbanks Alaska. Tributary of the Yukon river showing a good example of Oxbow Lakes "Left behind" by changes in the river flow. June 2005.

Finally, we head back to Anchorage airport for an Alaska Airlines 737-400 flight south on June 12th, landing at Vancouver enroute to San Francisco. We enjoyed three nights there but had one day driving south down the coast and coming back inland to Palo Alto to visit Bettie my second cousin who had moved over from New York some years back.

Our grand holiday comes to a close and we depart San Fran on Air NZ on June 15th on a 747-400 with flight time to Auckland of 12hrs 12mins and connect onto an Airbus A320 to Brisbane (A new type for me so see details below).

A really amazing trip!

Avro 748-2A

Avro built the 748 as a contender to replace the DC3 and it met with some success. Some 380 were built which did include an RAF version called the Andover. The 748 took to the air for the first time on June 24th, 1960 and a Series 1 was introduced into service by Skyways in 1961. This again was another aircraft using Rolls Royce Darts for its power plants. They could carry from 40 to 48 passengers.

C-FAGI was a Series 2A aircraft delivered in 1971 and operated by various Canadian airlines until it came to Air North in September 1998. Air North operated a combi version with freight in the forward part of aircraft and reduced seating usually for around 22 passengers in the rear.

Perhaps I should mention here that if the forward cargo area is very full, access from the rear to the cockpit for the cabin attendant has to be via a small door set down on the left side of the bulkhead. At least the front person in the "A" seat might get occasional in-flight entertainment!

Our flight on June 5th, 2005 was from Whitehorse in the Yukon via Dawson and Old Crow (a gravel strip inside the Arctic circle) and onto Fairbanks. Each of the three sectors was over an hour. This plane was still flying in 2016, but Air North now fly ATRs into Old Crow.

Photo shows the plane during the transit at Old Crow and the timber and Fibre Glass Batts just unloaded through the front freight door.

Avro 748's are available to view in the following countries: UK, Thailand, Australia, Sri Lanka, Brazil and Ecuador.

Avro 748-2A June 2005. During transit at Old Crow inside Arctic Circle.

Airbus A320-200

This might be considered a late entrant into the narrow body short/medium range airliner market compared say to the 737 which first flew some twenty years earlier but it was bristling with newer technology, such as fly by wire controls, and has sold extremely well to the extent it has now built close to 10,000 units which is not far behind Boeings tally in a far longer period.

The A320 can carry around 170 in a one class configuration but many variants have followed. The A321 is a stretched version which can carry up to 240.

The 319 and even smaller 318 cater to smaller passenger loads on less denser routes.

More recently, Airbus have brought out the 320 as an A320NEO which is much improved in terms of reduced fuel burn and better efficiency.

Our flight on ZK-OJH was Auckland to Brisbane on Jun 17th, 2005. This aircraft was withdrawn by air NZ in February, 2020 for storage in the USA.

OJH below flies in the colours of the "STAR ALLIANCE" of which Air New Zealand is a member and is shown courtesy of Rob Finlayson. A more typical Air NZ colour scheme although on a much smaller plane shows on the Embraer I flew in February 2002.

In all I've totalled up 19 sectors on A320s, six each with Jetstar and AIR NZ, four with LAN in South America and one each with Finnair, EasyJet and BA.

Airbus A320-200 June 2005. Photo courtesy of Rob Finlayson.

October to Longreach

Due to my interest in aircraft modelling which had become known in the travel industry, I had renovated models for TAA, Qantas and Atlantic Airways, but the major user had been Qantas, and one of the 747 captains who was also a founder of their museum out at Longreach in Queensland, asked me to renovate and rebuild several models, which are now displayed out there. As a reward for my services to the museum, Anne and I were flown out to Longreach to visit the museum.

19 October, we departed Brisbane on a DASH8-200 aircraft so this is a new type and details are below. Flight travels via Blackall so we remain on-board during a 14mins stop and then arrive at Longreach.

We have three nights there which allows us time to visit the museum and see my work and the other exhibits. Also, we boarded the Qantas 747-200 that was the main feature there at the time, and in the relaxed atmosphere of not working on a Panam turnaround, I learnt more about the nooks and crannies of a 747 in 30mins than the four years with Panam!

On our other day, we visited the Stockmen's Hall of Fame and to be honest whilst I'm not a 'museum' man, this was an excellent place to visit. Naturally, we include a visit to an outback pub while we were there!

Flight back on October 22nd, was on another Dash 8, this time non-stop, flight time 1hr 59mins.

De Havilland Canada DHC Dash 8-200

This was built as a regional airliner and the initial 100, then 200-series, both carried 40 passengers on the power of two Pratt and Whitney turboprop engines. First flight was on June 20th, 1983 and went into service with NorOntair in 1984. Boeing bought out the company then Bombardier then Longview but they revived the DHC brand name.

The aircraft was developed from the DASH7 four engined STOL plane but dispensing with the short take off performance and only utilising two engines. Stretched versions such as the 300 could carry up to 56 passengers and the 400 up to 90 have followed. In all 1249 units have been built as of June 2018.

VH-SDA was first flown in 1998 under a US registration not taken up by the airline so came out and joined the Qantas Group.

Our flight was on October 19th, 2005 Brisbane-Blackall-Longreach.

This aircraft left from Australia to Canada in 2014 and is now with Air Greenland under the Danish registration OY-GRO.

In all, I've flown on seven Dash 8 sectors. 5 sectors with Qantas in Australia, one with Air NZ and one with Wideroe in Norway. Photo shows SDA taken on Lord Howe Island as it happened to be the same aircraft that flew us to/from the island around a year after the Longreach trip.

De Havilland Canada DHC Dash 8-200 October 2005. Photo taken at Lord Howe Island in December next year when we flew in same aircraft.

2006

Christmas 2006

If you haven't got snow and cosy fires, I can't think of a better place than Lord Howe Island to spend a Christmas! It's located around 380 miles east of Australia about a third of the way towards New Zealand. Accommodation is limited to 400 people at any one time, and there are very few cars and most people hire a bike to get around.

As a result, the beaches wherever you go are virtually deserted and with lack of cars around, I found it reminiscent of my earliest holiday just after WW2! Such a tranquil place. If travel permits you should try and visit this magical place!

This photo shows Mt. Gower to the right the highest point on the island at 2871ft high, and Mt Lidgbird is alongside. Lidgbird looks higher because it is quite a bit nearer the camera. A guided walk takes you up Mt Gower which has its own micro climate on the top as it's often shrouded in low cloud.

The term 'Guided Walk' is a loose term. If you look at the photo, those slopes are pretty steep and it's a fairly rugged day 'walk'. Anyway, this sixty-four year-old managed it, but some of my younger companions seemed to struggle. Maybe my cycling keeps me fit!

Lord Howe Island. December 2006. It's hard not to get a great photo of this amazing destination!

The lagoon here is where the Short Sandringham flying boats coming from Rose Bay in Sydney would alight until the early 1970s.

I tried to get a seat on such a flight on my trip down under in 1971 but was unsuccessful! They finished operating in 1974 and now Dash 8 aircraft land on an 886 m long runway which stretches across the narrow middle neck of the island.

From where the photo is taken, is roughly where all the accommodation is located and the island is around 10 kms long and 2 kms at its widest point and roughly boomerang shaped. The steepness of the slopes on Mt. Gower prevented pigs on the island getting to the plateau like top on which a few Lord Howe Wood hen had taken refuge.

The pigs and vermin are now under control and the Wood hen are now in substantial numbers around the island. The coral reefs off the island are the most southerly in the world. As well as tourism, there is a thriving Kentia Palm industry on the island exporting plants worldwide for indoor locations.

The flight from Brisbane is SE to Lord Howe some 459 miles distant and flight time was 1hr 33mins on December 24th. The return was on December 31st, and both legs were on the same plane (SDA) that had flown us out to Longreach in October, the previous year.

2007

May

This was planned to be a big round world retirement trip starting just after my sixty-fifth birthday, however, you can blame it on me for not happening! I had been suffering from sleep apnoea, which in turn had created insomnia for Anne. She decided she was wasn't up to a trip that year, so I asked if I could travel to Antarctica later in the year, which I knew would be something she wouldn't want to do.

She gave me the okay to do that, so I started to do some research. I had wanted to see Emperor Penguins but they are further south into Antarctica, hence longer trips and more dollars in cost. I elected to see King penguins in the Falkland Islands which are only slightly smaller and gave me the added bonus of a visit there! The trip started in November.

November to South America/Antarctica

3 November, I head off from Brisbane to Auckland on an Air NZ 747-400 and stay one night. I hired a car and head up to NW Auckland and stay with old neighbours of ours and next morning, I delivered to our old house (photo shown in the 1975 year), the photos of the house being transported from the builder's yard by road to our plot. They showed us round the house which had virtually tripled in size with many extensions.

4 November, I departed Auckland on Aerolineas Argentinas Airbus A340-200. This is a new type so see details below. Arrived Buenos Aires same day having crossed the date line but arrived somewhat late in the afternoon, so missed out on seeing the colourful buildings of La Boca which I'd planned to do. I stayed the night then had to pick up some documents next morning. What I saw of the city, it is certainly a very vibrant and exciting place to visit!

Late afternoon, I boarded out of the city airport Jorge Newberry an MD83 operated by Austral Lineas Aereas a subsidiary of Aerolineas and flew down to El Calafate in the south.

I stayed there two nights, and on the full day had a day trip out to the Perito Merino Glacier.

Guanaco a wild animal related to the Llama living in Patagonia. Taken on the trip through Torres del Paine NP. November 2007.

The Towers! Sunrise at Torres Del Paine NP. November 2007.

Following El Calafate, I left on what is a day trip into Chile but many people such as me, use it on a one-way basis to take them to Torres Del Paine NP. Some of the day is spent touring the park, and a photo I've included previous page is of a Guanaco taken from the bus.

These are one of two wild animals found in Patagonia closely related to the Llama. The other is the Vicuna which lives at higher altitudes. I had two nights in the park at a hostel there, and with other people climbed on a day hike to a vantage point for lunch and then returned back to the hostel. One photo I've included was taken at sunrise of the famed towers.

Then headed for Punta Arenas all this by bus by the way. Getting to the main road from the hostel to get the bus I'm reminded we all had to get off the hostel shuttle bus and walk across the bridge to lighten the load. That's one photo sadly I didn't capture! Stayed one night at Punta Arenas which is my jumping off point for the Falklands.

Next morning, the 10th November, LAN the Chilean Airline have a flight comes down from Santiago, stops at Punta arenas in the south of Chile then heads to the Falklands. This ran weekly but I happened to pick the Sat each way in the month when it went via Rio Gallagos (RG) in Argentina.

This used to be a refuelling stop from Buenos Aires to Auckland or Sydney when earlier jets didn't have the range to do it non-stop. However, before I board the plane, there are two boarding queues at the airport with no signage to say I should be in either one, so I joined the right-hand queue. Got talking to a lady and she asked me how long I was going to Antarctica for, so I said eleven days.

Conversation went on for a minute or two until it dawned on her I was in the wrong queue! She was travelling on an Ilyushin IL76 aircraft outside on the tarmac on summer work at Patriot Hills in Antarctica, I should be in the left queue going to the Falklands! I know my aircraft but others have got on the wrong planes.

Well, Lan showed up with their Airbus A320 and flight time to RG was 22 mins then to Mount Pleasant the long-haul airport serving Port Stanley in the Falklands, 1hr 2mins.

Remembrance Day Service Port Stanley East Falkland 11th Nov 2007.
Also, marked the twenty-fifth anniversary of the British victory in the 1982 Falklands war.

When we landed, there were quite a few large jets there, DC10's and the like and it turned out it was the twenty-fifth anniversary of the British victory in the Falklands war, and many veterans had come down from UK to be part of the remembrance service next day.

So, next morning I attended the Remembrance Day service and photo is shown taken on the day, and two Tornados did a flypast at 11 AM down Port Stanley sound. How fortunate was I to pick such a date? I had friends of friends in the Falklands so saw a great deal more than perhaps I otherwise would have.

But I joined regular day trips to see the King Penguins at Volunteer Beach (see photo) and another to Kidney Cove where I saw a number of other Penguin species. During the week, I saw another cruise ship called the Explorer, which I'd been considering travelling on which visited South Georgia as well as the Antarctic peninsula. The fact of that becomes relevant a bit later.

The week went too quickly, there was so much to see. My accommodation was a sequel to the Falklands war. The British needed to increase their military numbers after the end of the war, so these container accommodation units housed construction workers helping to build extra for the troops. It was only a short walk out of town but very reasonable in cost.

Lookout Lodge just out of Port Stanley. Used for construction workers after the 1982 conflict. This was my accommodation. November 2007

King Penguins at Volunteer beach on East Falkland. November 2007.

On November 17th, I left Falkland on a LAN A320 again via RG flight times 1hr 10mins, then 29mins to land in Punta Arenas for one night.

Next day, it was a bus south to Ushuaia. This was a big day on the bus and also a great display of Patagonian winds at their best. Arrived there into light snowfall and had two nights of my own accommodation before joining the Cruise package which included one more night's hotel before cruise ship departure the next day.

THE ANTARCTIC CRUISE

Wednesday, November 21st, we leave port on our cruise ship the MV Lyubov Orlova (named after the Russian actress) with ice strengthened hull and tonnage of 4251, and headed across the Drake Passage to the Antarctic Peninsula. They call it the Drake Shake or the Drake lake. We had both! Following morning, photo shows which version we had.

The Drake Passage! November 2007.

Now this bit gets weird. Into the second day and word is spreading that a ship in Antarctica is in trouble and is sinking, and in summer there are plenty of cruise ships down there, but are asked to changed course slightly to render assistance if necessary. The vessel in trouble is MV Explorer, the ship I saw in the Falklands so I could have been on it but that isn't it!

I'm thinking of Anne and to break up the time while I was away I booked Anne and her friend, Jan, on a fly/drive to NZ. I needed to call them and looked up their itinerary to see which motel I needed to call.

Sit back for this one! They were in Te Anau in the alps in the South Island staying at the EXPLORER motel! A fellow cruiser who I am still in touch with, got me to use her satellite phone and we spoke to the motel owners, and assured them my vessel was alive and well! They said Anne and Jan were out for the day at Milford sound and would get the message on their return.

Crazy people swimming at Deception Island Antarctica! Yours truly on right! Water temp +2C! November 2007.

Now whilst we are on the subject of water at +2 C, mention should be made of an amazing man by the name of Lewis Pugh, who can meditate his body into a state whereby he can sustain cold water temperatures for prolonged periods. He swims in frigid waters all over the world, but in this particular case, if you look at the photo I've included, he swam from one side of the Caldera 1.6 kms to the other side in just over 30mins in +2 C!

If you want more on all his incredible swims see his website Lewispugh.com.

A visit to Half Moon island provided this encounter with an Adele penguin.

Adele penguin Antarctica using built in tobogganing equipment! November 2007.

The photo with the Zodiac in it was taken just over 65 degrees south at Petermann Island, which is as far south as we travelled. A more pristine place it would be hard to imagine.

Zodiac at Petermann Island just over 65 degrees South. I think this shot reflects the space and solitude of Antarctica. November 2007.

Antarctica is a magnificent place and we landed twice on the continent itself as opposed to Islands. Our first landing was at the Argentinian station Almirante Brown in Paradise Bay and second was at Neko harbour in photo below.

Neko Harbour. Our last landing on the continent before return across the Drake passage.
The Penguins are Gentoo which are the fastest swimmers of all the species. November 2007.

Finally, after two days back on the Drake lake, this time quite smooth, we arrived into Ushuaia on December 1st.

The flight back up from Ushuaia is to the main Pistarini (EZE) international airport in Buenos Aires on an Aerolineas 737-500 flight time 3hrs 18mins.

Next day, I really walked around the city but still missing La Boca but my flight was delayed further into the early hours of the next day.

3 December, again from Pistarini departed on an Aerolineas A340-200 heading towards Auckland. This would be the one and only time I've fallen asleep on an aircraft while we were taxiing out! As we lined up onto the runway and the engines started to spool up that woke me up with a start!

Then whilst I saw the dawn just breaking, I must have fallen asleep again and when I awoke we were only a bit south of NZ, still with small bergs in the water, and I saw from the flight track on the back of the seat rest that we had been far to the south of where I'd been at Petermann Island and I'd been asleep!

At Auckland, I transferred to an adjacent gate onto an Air NZ 777-200 back to Brisbane.

That was truly an amazing trip!

Airbus A340-200

This was developed with experience from the A300, and this and the A330 use the same fuselage cross section as the earlier jet. It was a true long-haul airliner with the 200-series carrying 250 passengers in three classes over a stage length of 6700 nmi.

However, with many stretches and changes a 300, 500 and 600-series were developed to the extent the 600 could carry 370 passengers over a stage length of 7800 nmi. However, the 500 was a shorter version, so carried a lesser number of passengers but could achieve a stage length of 9000 nmi.

First flight of the 200 was on October 25th, 1991 with the plane entering service both with Lufthansa and Air France on March 15th, 1993. Airbus have built 380 of the A340 when production ended.

LV-ZPX was originally delivered to Cathay Pacific in February 1995 then to Philippine Airlines two years later in February 1997, then it came to Aerolineas Argentinas in July 1999.

My flight on this aircraft was from Auckland to Buenos Aires on November 4th, 2007.

This plane continued flying with that airline until 2014 but is now stored at Victorville in USA. Photo is of sister ship ZPJ which took 13hrs 17mins to fly back from South America to Auckland, my longest flight. Photo taken from AIR NZ 777 just pushing back on my flight home to Brisbane.

I have flown three A340 sectors, the two Aerolineas sectors plus a sector with Finnair from Hong Kong to Helsinki in the following year.

Airbus A340-200 Auckland-Buenos Aires November 2007. Taken of LV-ZPJ, plane used on return journey on arrival, my longest flight.

2008

July to UK

Initially, we should have left in June, but late May, Anne ended up in Hospital for four nights with some inner ear infection, so after great problems with insurance, and touch and go with medical clearance, we were able to depart in July. The plan was Anne and her friend, Val, would do a river cruise Budapest to Amsterdam whilst I spent my time touring the Scottish Islands many of which I had not visited before.

We departed Brisbane on July 10th on a Qantas Airbus A330 (a new type so see details below) and arrived Hong Kong, this time landing at the new airport at Chep Lap Kok built on fresh land west of Hong Kong city. We stayed at an airport hotel overnight and returned next morning for onward flight with Finnair. It was scheduled to be an MD11 (a development from the DC10) but an Airbus A340-300 taxied into the gate and flight time to Helsinki was 10hrs 7mins.

Our original itinerary had been for a three-night stay but this new one gave us two nights but I was still able to show the girls around the highlights of the city, and in the afternoon, hired a car and headed east to the lovely timbered town of Porvoo nearer to the Russian border. Back to Helsinki and visited the Jean Sebelius park just to the NW of the city before reaching our hotel for our second night.

Next morning, used the car to take us to the airport north of the city and got the girls off on their flight down to Budapest. I had a slightly later flight to LHR on a Finnair A320 and my sister, Elaine, and husband met me and I stayed with them for a week visiting the Farnborough Air show of course!

On July 20th, I departed Luton airport on an Easyjet Airbus A319 (a new type so see details below) and landed at Abbotsinch Airport Glasgow which had replaced the old Renfrew airport I used to fly to in the 1960s.

Jeff (Dark top) and yours truly in recent photo. My cycling buddy for many of my teen years to a vast number of UK airfields we visited.

I then took a train down to Prestwick and had lunch with Stewart (from the old Prestwick aviation days) and his wife. Last time I'd seen them was back on a UK trip with Panam!

Now in all my trips to the Prestwick area, the view out to the west over the Firth of Clyde had the Isle of Arran looking as a very alluring place to visit. The highest point on the Island is Goat fell at 2866ft, just to the north of Brodick about halfway up the east side and this is where the ferry calls in from the mainland.

This trip gave me the chance to go over to Arran, and Stewart dropped me off at Ardrossan the mainland port, and I took an evening ferry over to Brodick and stayed the night. Early next morning, I did an ascent of Goat Fell and was on the summit just after 10 AM and back in Brodick by 1 PM. Then a ferry back to Ardrossan an hour later for a night there and next morning, a train up to

Abbotsinch airport Glasgow to fly out on the BA flight to Barra at southern end of the Western Isles.

BA 'Twotter' G-BVVK is probably one of the most photographed aircraft in the world. Barra is considered one of the ten most dangerous airports in the world and when they are showing footage of the 'airport' on media, 'VVK' inevitably is the plane they show!

Interestingly, while they park these planes at a normal gate on the mainland, they do not push them back with an aircraft tug. The pilots use reverse thrust to push back from the gate make a 90 degree turn to end up pointing in the correct direction to taxi towards the runway! That's an exciting start to a journey in itself!

Well on this occasion we take off at 1427 and land back at Glasgow at 1638! Flight time of 2hrs 11mins. We held overhead Barra for 25mins and tried two approaches but due low cloud could not land and had to divert back to Glasgow! Had a night at a hotel and went back the next day, this time got there after a flight of 51mins.

In travel photos, you will see image of our plane in front, plus the scheduled flight for the day having landed a few minutes after us. That is a fairly rare shot to have the two 'Twotters' together on the beach.

I make my way up the Western Isles enjoying beautiful scenery and beaches which wouldn't be out of place in a Caribbean brochure and see Harris Tweed being made and arrive in Stornoway. I make sure to visit the famed Callinish stones where there was a large school party making things a bit crowded.

I'd been there about 10mins when the school teacher said, "Let's go to the gift shop and get an ice Cream," and I replied "Why didn't I think of that!" I then got the photos I wanted!

Next day, July 26th I depart Stornoway to get to the Orkneys. I wanted to go via Inverness (a bit of a short cut) but the flights didn't work that day, so took a slightly longer route down via Glasgow with a BA Saab 340, flight time 47mins, then north to Kirkwall in the Orkney Islands in another Saab 340, flight time 51mins. I had two nights in Stromness and on first evening, there was a street parade through town so a lucky bonus for me.

Next day, I travelled over to the island of Hoy across Scapa Flow which has been used by the British Navy as a safe northern anchorage area, and was the scene at the end of WW1 of the scuttling of ships of the German Navy.

After my second night, back in Stromness, I returned to Kirkwall airport for an onward journey to the Shetlands.

This was July 28th, and my flight had an STD of 1110 but the aircraft I was due to leave on was just leaving to go down south to Inverness. That's never a good sign but things were delayed due to summer fog.

Eventually, we departed on the BA Saab 340 at 1347 just over 2.5hrs late. Normally, the blocks to blocks time for this sector is 35mins, so well under 30mins in the air allowing for taxy times even at small Scottish airports being short. We were in the air for 48mins.

On approaching Sumburgh Airport in Shetland on runway 27, we had to overshoot due to the low visibility but on climbing out at the far end it was brilliant sunshine, so Capt. Anderson did a smooth 180 degree turn and landed on runway 09. The alternative would have been to go to an airfield up in the north of Shetland called Scatsta which can take small jets like Bae146's and was used for Oil field support work.

I enjoyed three nights in Lerwick, the capital of Shetland and first full day enjoyed out on an island called Noss, to the east of Lerwick under the protection of the RSPB (Royal Society for Protection of Birds), and saw huge numbers of Gannets, some seals and got reunited with Puffins.

Second full day I ventured north to a spot called "Mavis Grind" which is a narrow strip of land separating the North Sea from the Atlantic Ocean. Here the Vikings used to portage their longboats over the ground from one water the 50 m to the other, rolling them on logs. There is a road sign as you approach which must be a pretty rare one saying 'Otters Crossing'.

It is now July 31st, and I now head to London first a BA Saab 340 to Aberdeen then connect onto a BA Airbus A319 to LHR.

I picked up a hire car and join Anne who had finished her river cruise in Amsterdam and now arrived in UK and spent the day with friends of hers, and we then arrive at my sister's house. As well as time there with my sister, we used it as a base for several tours around the UK to see friends and relatives, but one included the sites where our family's caravan was sighted along the south coast when I was a youngster, and I also got to ride again on the Romney Hythe Dymchurch railway!

On September 8th, we departed from LHR on a Qantas 747-400 to Singapore flight time 12hrs 13mins, and connected on arrival onto an Airbus A330 from

Singapore to Brisbane arriving AM on the 10th. We came a long way but rode in a Jetstream.

We left Singapore 7mins late arrived Brisbane 7mins early, came overhead Ayers rock (now Uluru) which is a much longer way to come than a great circle route but at times the speed readout on the seat back recorded speed over the ground at 682 mph.

That was a great trip but at two months away, we felt it was a little too long.

Airbus A330-300

This wide body twin jet airliner was a development from the earlier A300. It first flew on November 2nd, 1992 and was introduced into airline service by Air Inter around fourteen months later on January 17th, 1994. It could carry 277 passengers in the 300-series, but a shorter version which was termed the 200-series followed in 1998.

Later, further development created the A330NEO and this was introduced to airline service by TAP, the Portuguese airline, in December, 2018. Overall, as of June 2021, Airbus have built 1518 of the A330.

VH-QPC first flew with Qantas on January 28th, 2004. My flight from Brisbane to Hong Kong was on July 10th, 2008. This plane was still in use with Qantas as of August 2021.

I have flown a total of four sectors on A330s, two each with Qantas and SQ.

Airbus A330-300 July 2008. Prior to departure from Brisbane.

Airbus A319-100

This is a shortened variant of the A320 and first flew August 25th, 1995 and introduced to airline service by Swissair in April 1996. It could carry between 124 to 156 passengers and maximum range is 3700 nmi. Some 1486 A319 have been built to date and a NEO version is now available, but not in as much demand as sales for the 320 version.

G-EZAX, the aircraft I flew on, was delivered to EasyJet in July 2006. My flight was from Luton airport (London) to Glasgow on July 20th, 2008 with flight time 58mins.

This plane was withdrawn from use by EasyJet in February 2021 and transferred to United.

Photo below of a sister ship a few days later at Glasgow airport.

Have flown four A319 sectors, the above with EasyJet, one with TAP Portuguese airlines and two with BA.

Airbus A319-100 July 2008. Sister ship shown taxiing at Glasgow.

Barra Airport. A rare shot with my delayed flight from previous day in foreground and scheduled flight for the day just arrived behind. July 2008.

2009

November to NZ

This required a personal trip to New Plymouth in New Zealand where Amy, our daughter, was at the time. She needed some support so it was elected I should travel over and bring her home to Australia.

On November 18th, I departed on an Air NZ Airbus A320 from Brisbane to Wellington, and picked up a hire car there and drove around 4.5hrs up to New Plymouth, and met up with Amy and stayed there for two nights.

On November 20th, we departed on an Air NZ Dash 8 from New Plymouth to Auckland a flight of just 32mins and connected there onto a Qantas 737-400 back over to Brisbane.

2010

June to Sydney

Sadly, we had news from Sydney that Bill, Joyce's surviving husband, had passed away very suddenly. He was in his eighty-seventh year but had been in quite good health. We had seen him in the previous year on a car trip down there.

    I made a one night trip down to attend his funeral, and travelled down on a Virgin 737-700 on June 23rd and returned following day on a 737-800 of the same airline. He is still missed and he was an amazing character!

2011

March to Lady Elliot Island

My sister, Elaine, in UK has twin granddaughters who were finishing high school and taking a 'gap' year trip around the world. Part of it included staying with us for a few weeks, and early in the stay, partly because turtles were still hatching and there was a full moon, we took them up to Lady Elliot island (where we had taken their grandparents in 1987).

We drove up to Bundaberg about a five-hour drive north of Brisbane and stayed the night. This has the airport where you leave for the journey out to Lady Elliot from.

On March 20th, we departed on a SeaAir Britten Norman Islander to the island with flight time of 32mins. We did see the last of the turtle hatchlings heading for the water, and it was full moon so it was great to walk around the island even at night, do reef walking in the day and snorkelling. See below a photo I took on this trip of a Frigate Bird soaring in the breeze over the island. A two-night stay is far too short but gave them a taste of the barrier reef.

Frigate Bird soaring over Lady Elliot Island. March 2011.

Three days later, we flew back to Bundaberg, this time on a Sea Air Cessna Grand Caravan (this is a new type for me see details below).

Cessna 208b Grand Caravan

An aircraft from the Cessna company designed for smaller operators, generally flying shorter trips, often in remote areas, and can be used from semi prepared strips such as grass and gravel.

It was first flown on December 9th, 1982, and the cargo pod shown on the photo was introduced in 1986. Power was from a Pratt and Whitney turboprop engine usually of around 850 shp but slightly different engine powers were used throughout production which totalled 2600 units.

9 passengers were generally carried plus an extra in the right-hand pilot's seat. A high-density version could carry 13 but then 2 pilots would be carried.

VH-LMZ shown taken on an earlier take off from Lady Elliot was the plane I travelled in, and was built in 1989 and delivered to a US operator in February 1990. It then operated in Greenland and Norway until the late 1990s and arrived with Sea Air in Australia in September 1999 where the current registration was taken up.

Our flight was a return from Lady Elliot Island on Queensland's Barrier reef to Bundaberg on the mainland on March 22nd, 2011, a distance of 50 nmi taking 29mins. This time I was able to occupy the right-hand pilot's seat. This plane was still flying in Australia as of August 2021.

Cessna 208B Grand Caravan March 2011. Take off from Lady Elliott during our stay.

May a Flying Lesson!

Well, I really got into DIY today on my birthday, the 27th May. I went down to Gold Coast Airport, our local airport, where we normally fly out of to Sydney or Melbourne and more recently even to New Zealand, but this time I get into Cessna 172 VH-NWZ and go for a flying lesson!

I've since had a go on a 737 simulator but that's about the sum total of my hands-on experience.

Cessna 172R Skyhawk

This was developed from the smaller 170 model as a general aviation aircraft and has been an outstanding popular aircraft for the commercial use and private sector alike. Many a pilot has cut his teeth with his initial flight lessons on this airplane (at least I had one!).

The 170 first flew in 1948, and the 172 on June 12th, 1955. Originally, it had tailwheel (always affectionately known as a taildragger!) but was quickly changed to a tricycle undercarriage. It's a four-seater airplane and started with a 145 hp (horse power) but through production, various motors have been used even as high as 210 hp. The total number built is the huge number of 44,000!

VH-NWZ, the aircraft I had my flight lesson in, was built in 2000 and delivered on August 31st, 2000. My flight was out of Gold Coast airport on my sixty-ninth birthday on May 27th, 2011 and lasted for 42mins and I performed the landing! Photo shows yours truly alongside 'NWZ'. This planes still flying on the Gold Coast as of August 2021.

Cessna 172R Skyhawk Gold Coast Airport May 2011. My flying lesson!

September to NZ

We decided to go for a late winter trip to the Southern Alps of New Zealand. Brisbane enjoys non-stop flights to Queenstown set right in the middle of the Alps. It's a beautiful setting and is popular year-round for snow sports in the winter and summer activities too such as Bungy jumping, jet boat rides etc. and normal sight-seeing.

Annie Snow Shoeing in the Remarkables above Queenstown NZ. September 2011.

We departed on September 25th on Air NZ Airbus A320 Brisbane into Queenstown, flight time just 2hrs 58mins.

During our time there, we had hoped to do a helicopter excursion onto the Nevis Snowfield and do a Skidoo ride. My second try at doing this activity, but winter season had been short that year, so had stopped running at time we arrived. Instead, we opted to take a bus up to the Remarkables Ski field and went on a Snow shoe walk there.

Anne found it hard going but she managed it. We stopped for an afternoon snack on a frozen lake! Photo previous page shows Anne on the walk!

After Queenstown, we travelled to Manapouri on Lake TeAnau, and as we had both been to Milford Sound, on this trip we did a day excursion into Doubtful Sound which was equally impressive but not as frequently visited.

Following that, we travelled down to Invercargill, right down the foot of the South Island and enjoyed the sights around there before flying to Stewart Island.

On November 3rd, we departed Invercargill to Oban on Stewart Island Airways on a Britten Norman Islander, flight time 15mins.

Now the airstrip is out of town so passenger's check-in at the town office at Oban, and get taken out to the airstrip, wait for the arriving plane, bus and plane swop loads and head back to their respective destinations.

Earlier I had asked Stewart if he wanted to join us on Stewart island, but as he had been to UK in June and was due to go down to Christchurch for Christmas, he said he wouldn't join us so I said that was fine. Below is a photo of someone holding up a sign with my name on it when we landed! It turned out to be my brother! He had decided to turn up instead and surprise us!

Stewart's sign on Stewart Island NZ. October 2011.

I do get my own back on him twelve months later when we go to Cairns in November 2012.

Well, we had a great time on 'My Brothers Island'. We both go back to Invercargill on the 7th November, he by ferry to Bluff/Invercargill, and our flight back was on the same BN Islander as the flight over and I had the right-hand pilots seat.

We picked up my brother in Invercargill, and we all drove to Dunedin and spent a night there, before we see him off at the airport back to the North Island.

We enjoyed a further two nights in Dunedin (dubbed the Edinburgh of the South with a distinct Scottish flavour). We toured the Otago Peninsula and also climbed Baldwin St, claimed to be the steepest street in the world, where at one point it is 1 in 2.86 gradient!

We motored north up the east coast after that, breaking our journey in a couple of places, and finally having some nights with my nephew, Mark (my brother's youngest son who lives just south of Christchurch). After staying with them, we went up to Christchurch airport for our flight home.

On November 13th, we departed Christchurch on an Air NZ Airbus A320 to Brisbane flight time 3hrs 23mins, the end of a really great holiday!

2012

February Start with Care Flight

After our return from NZ, a good friend of mine told me about a Medical Rescue organisation called Care Flight, using mainly helicopters based at Gold Coast airport. They were looking for volunteers to show tour groups round their hanger facility, and explain how they operated etc.

I applied to go on the training course together with about ten other people, and around May of 2012, we started in earnest showing groups around the hanger, where there would usually be a Bell 412 ready and waiting to be called out. It was very unusual to run a tour without an aircraft there at all. We also had a Lear jet based there which was used for short haul overseas rescues such as from Fiji, Vanuatu etc.

In fact, I contributed to Care Flight a 1 m long model of one of the Lear jets which I made, which is still at the entrance to the hanger at one of the Brisbane airports (the smaller one called Archerfield where the helicopter maintenance is now done). Please see below photo of a typical tour in progress in the Gold Coast hanger.

Sadly, as I mentioned maintenance got moved to Brisbane but also the Gold Coast base closed, and all operations are now conducted from Brisbane International airport. The name was also changed to Lifeflight. but I will include another photo and text later to mark the finale to my time with the organisation.

The start of the Care Flight Hanger tours May 2012.

November to Cairns

Well, Cairns was beckoning for two reasons. There was a total solar eclipse coming up in mid-November, which passed across the Queensland Coast midway between Cairns and Port Douglas. This gave us a good chance to try out the Ellis Beach accommodation, plus this is the time the Buff Breasted Paradise Kingfisher starts arriving down from Papua New Guinea for the summer months.

A magnificent looking Kingfisher with a long-plumed tail. One that was on my list to see! My brother Stewart is to join us from NZ.

Anne and I flew up on November 10th, Brisbane to Cairns on a Qantas 737-800, hired a car and drove up to Ellis beach which as I've mentioned before could be anyway on a tropical island. We have five nights booked there.

I had to return next morning to Cairns airport to change the car, as there was a fault and we had it for two weeks, and will be driving all the way south to home in it, but not only that, I needed to pick up my brother, who due to flight changes, had to spend a night in Sydney enroute and arrived one day later.

Well what comes next is my encore to the Stewart Island surprise. I kept the sign and added a PS, so when he arrived down the arrivals walkway at Cairns terminal, he was greeted by a sign which said, 'HYSLOP welcome to my Island! PS Mine's bigger than yours!'

We enjoyed our nights on Ellis beach (it was so much better than Tahiti in 1976!) and fortunately, the clouds cleared just in time for us to enjoy the eclipse around 8 AM on morning of November 14th, the centre of the track was only about 6 miles north of where we were staying so it was just the right location.

Stewart and I did a Barrier Reef trip out of Port Douglas to a pontoon but despite wearing lycra protective gear, I got stung by a stinger on my upper lip, which was about the only exposed portion of my body. It was very stressful at the time and put a dampener on the rest of the day.

On November 15th, we left Ellis Beach and drove up to the Atherton Tablelands to a property called Jullaten, which is basically a bird watching lodge, and we spent three nights there, and did indeed see the Paradise Kingfishers on most mornings, although good photos were hard to get.

After our stay, we had seven nights to work our way down the Queensland coast to come home to our house on the Gold Coast. Some of them were two night stays including Mackay, where we spent the day up at Eungella NP and saw Duck Billed Platypus in the rivers and ponds up there. So, we arrived home November 25th, and then fare welled my brother off to NZ.

2013

April to Northern Territory
Eclipse Time Again!

This time there is an annular eclipse (see photo next pages). On this occasion, the moon is too far away from the earth to totally block out the sun, but does create a perfect ring but the photo I've shown is at the start of that process. So, this eclipse is in early May north of Alice Springs.

This is an area that Anne and I have never been to, so we head off to the Northern Territory. As we needed an early flight out of Sydney, we travelled down the day before.

On April 30th, we departed Gold Coast on Virgin 737-800 to arrive Sydney. Another passenger picked up Anne's bag, so it will be sometime before it's returned to the airport. I wasn't keen on claiming it next morning prior to our flight, so I returned same evening to pick it up.

I have always had readily identifiable bags. One was a green Bag with a big 'N' on one side and a 'Y' on the other. I wasn't game on putting NY on the one side in case someone put it on a flight to New York! Oh by the way, NY means NOT YOURs!

However, my current bag is a Red bag with the stars of the Southern Cross on it, and I photographed it whilst it was going across the apron on a baggage cart! Please don't travel with a black bag! It makes tracking it that much harder if it gets lost.

Ayers Rock (now Uluru) at sunset. May 2013.

Start of the Annular Eclipse Northern Territory. May 2013.

1 May, we left from Sydney on a Virgin 737-800, flight time 3hrs 8mins to Ayers Rock Airport which serves the nearby town of Yulara. Before we even got to the terminal, we see all these folks waving at us. Do we know anyone here? This is all explained by the first thing we did.

When we got into town, we each bought fly screen hats to keep the flies away! We had three nights here, and first full day we headed to the Rock but it was too windy to climb. I should point out at the time in 2013, whilst the Aboriginal Custodians of Ayers Rock (now called Uluru) discouraged climbing of the rock, it was not banned but left to your personal choice. There is now a ban on climbing in place.

As an alternative, we drove west to the Olgas about one hour's journey each way and spend the day out there. They feature some very smooth rock formations standing high out of otherwise flat terrain. One evening we went out to see the setting sun on Ayers Rock, and although, I took 14 photos, only one had the really 'reddish' glow that's shows on previous page.

I guess the sun must be at a specific angle to create that effect for just a minute or so, if that each day.

Following day, although, it was windy at the start, delaying start of a climb, late morning I started the climb of the Rock and got around 95% of the way up, but was running out of water so made a judgement call to turn around where I did. When I got to the base I realised here was a water tank to top up bottles which I could have used before I set off!

After our three nights, we drove towards Alice Springs about a six-hour journey NE, and stopped in at a Camel ranch on the way, and each got a ride on a "Ship of the Desert!"

We had three nights in Alice which is not long enough but we saw as much as we could in the time, including the Royal Flying Doctor Headquarters which included a full mock-up of their main workhorse which is the Swiss built Pilatus PC12 aircraft.

Now on May 7th, we drop off the car and pick up a Motorhome for a drive up to Darwin.

We were supposed to pick up a Toyota Hi-Ace but they said we have upgraded you to the Mercedes Sprinter, which is like the bigger models with one of the beds in a bubble over the driver's cabin. Anne took one look at it and said she couldn't drive it, but once out onto the highway, she soon got used to it.

And by two days later, had found a spot where other Motorhomes are parked at a layby which is only a few kms south of where we needed to be next morning for the eclipse. Normally, Anne wouldn't 'free camp' but there was safety in numbers here.

Next morning, we left early for the few kms north to be in the right spot which is the centreline of where the eclipse will track across the road. GPS is so accurate that within 20ft I could tell whether I was one side or the other of the centre line! I duly got a series of photos and one I've shown I think best illustrates the process of the moon passing in front of the sun.

We kept heading north including Katherine Gorge, then two nights in Kakadu NP seeing Crocs again, finally arriving in Darwin and dropping off the Motorhome. After some nights in Darwin seeing the sights there, we hired a car for two nights, down to Litchfield NP where there are some amazing pools you can take a dip in (no crocs).

Then May 22nd, drove back up to Darwin airport to fly home, this time on Qantas 767-300 to Brisbane flight time 3hrs 30mins. A pretty memorable holiday!

PS—Many major airlines were disposing of older types, and this Qantas 767 we have just flown on would be no exception as it was in its 21st year of flying. It's last flight for Qantas was in December of the following year, by which time it had done over 26000 flights. It was still flying in DHL colours as of September 2020.

2014

January

First I should mention a trip we didn't make! I had been having some stomach problems which were not getting better, so finally on the evening prior to the trip (15 January), we cancelled the trip. In all the checks and tests the doctor decided to do, he asked me had I ever had a Heart Echo Cardiogram to which I replied, "No".

I was put on medication for the stomach disorder, then the Cardiogram came back with a problem with the Aorta in my heart, so by the time I was cleared for an exploratory to find out what was going on in the stomach, there was nothing there to find. The medication had done its job in the meantime! Meanwhile I was put on an annual watch for the aorta problem which surfaces later on in five years' time!

June to Sydney

My namesake (Graham Hyslop) in Sydney, some two years older than me, had been in ill health for a number of years, but finally in early 2014, it became only a matter of time before he would pass but we did have an indication from his son down there, it was expected to be around July.

We planned a trip to visit him and go onto the Snowy Mountains and we had tickets to go down around June 20th. However, after talking to his son on morning of the 4th, when things were still reasonably OK (as with my own father years earlier), we missed a text that evening saying he had passed away.

It was only on Tuesday, the next week, I rang to check on progress, I found out the sad news and that the funeral was in two days' time. Qantas as usual did the right thing and brought our tickets forward to the next day with minimal fee.

On June 11th, we departed Gold Coast on Qantas 737-800 to arrive Sydney. Anne's brother, David, plus my cousin, Evelyn, plus Graham's family also resided on the north side of Sydney, so we based ourselves there for our five night stay.

Following day was the funeral service and I must say it is very strange to walk into a church and see your name up in large letters with your date of passing! Everybody at the church and the wake knew who I was because facially we looked alike. There are some family genes there somewhere! I got to meet up with his son, Karl, again who had flown down from Stockholm and I had met him and his wife there on my 1999 trip.

As it was too early in the snow season to go down to the 'snowies', we headed up to the Blue Mountains which we really enjoyed, and then returned to Sydney for a flight home.

On June 20th, we departed Sydney on Virgin 737-800 to the Gold Coast.

Graham was a great family man and a true friend, and I still have fond memories of the times when we could meet up.

November to NZ

Anne enjoyed the motorhome trip to the Northern Territory. For twelve days, we had our own wheels and only unpacked the once. Bit like a cruise on land! We decided to head to NZ and do another one. Sometimes you can get a cheap rate taking one northbound from Christchurch to Auckland, as most tourists start in Auckland and take them south creating a stockpile of vans down in the South Island.

However, on this occasion a cheaper cost repositioning one north didn't come into the offer but, for the large size van we got it was still about the same price as the small van we would have had in the Northern Territory.

We departed from Gold Coast Airport over to NZ on November 6th, on Jetstar (a low-cost branch of Qantas) on an Airbus A320, flight time 3hrs 1min, to Christchurch. Initially, we had three nights there and saw the city reshaping itself after its devastating earthquake, including a replacement 'Cardboard Cathedral' made of huge six-foot diameter cardboard tubes laid into rows to make an a frame building.

It did look modern and magnificent. On a corner plot in the city, there are 185 white chairs of all shapes and sizes including baby chairs and strollers to reflect all those that lost their lives in the quake.

On second day, we departed on a train day trip, the "Trans Alpine Express" which travels to the west coast to Greymouth but as we had already been there on our 1991 trip, we stopped halfway for the day at Arthurs Pass and climbed up to a magnificent waterfall and enjoyed some hours around the village, waiting for the return of the train to get us back to Christchurch.

We then picked up a motorhome and drove down south of the city to Mark, Stewart's youngest son, where Stewart had been staying, visiting from the north island. After two nights, we dropped Stewart at the airport for his flight north, and then continued up the east coast stopping at the famed Kaikoura to do a whale watching trip.

Then continued up to Picton and took the motorhome over on the Ferry to Wellington. Too complicated to unpack motorhomes but car hires stay on their respective islands.

We travelled north from Wellington and made out way up to Mt Ruapehu in Tongariro NP in the centre on the North Island.

My brother travelled up from his home in Hawkes bay to join us. We had been here in July when we lived in Auckland, and Anne and I had a brief introduction to skiing (with a modicum of success!). Well this was November, so it was still plenty cool and snow still around.

We moved north round the east side of Lake Taupo next day to stay two nights in Taupo town, and enjoyed the sights there once more, and even paid money and went into the real De Brett's spa instead of using their outfall water at the lakeside! My Scottish blood must be thinning a bit!

After that, Stewart headed back home and we stayed a night with Ken and Marnie in Tauranga.

Then to Cooks beach on the Coromandel Peninsula. Some magnificent scenery here plus some thermal pools on the beach where you can have a good soak.

Finally, we head to Auckland where we dropped the motorhome and traded for a hire car. Even though we had booked ahead, we had great trouble finding a room. Even the roads were jammed. There was a Rolling Stones concert on! We had three nights here mainly catching up with Mike and Jill who had been old neighbours opposite our house in NW Auckland.

Finally, November 25th, we departed from Auckland on Virgin 737-800 again straight into Gold Coast.

A really great trip!

2015

August to Adelaide

Well Mike and Jill from Auckland were coming to Australia. They flew to Darwin and caught the famous "Ghan" train down through Alice Springs to Adelaide.

It stops for periods of time along the way allowing passengers time to see Katherine Gorge, have time in Alice Springs and also time for tours in the Opal mining town further south at Coober Pedy where a great many people live in underground homes to escape the summer heat. We headed down to Adelaide a few days ahead of the train's arrival, as there was an air museum I wanted to visit plus an aero modelling show also on!

We left Gold Coast on August 15th, on a Virgin 737-800 and flight time was 2hrs 21 mins to Adelaide. We enjoyed Adelaide over the weekend, visiting the things Anne and I wanted to do, and then met up with Mike and Jill when the Ghan rolled in a few days later.

We then toured together the rest of the week seeing as much as we could within the limited time. It included a day out down to the south coast to Victor Harbour which is a great place for a visit with a horse drawn Tram out to an island along a causeway out from the town.

On our last shared day together, which was the Friday of the week, I'd managed to get us a booking on a lunchtime cruise on a Stern Wheeler the "Proud Mary" on the Murray River out to the east of Adelaide, which rounded off our stay really well, and we travelled back through the German influenced town of Hahndorf on our way back to Adelaide.

Flight to the Gold Coast left too early the next day for our liking (or at least Anne's) so we opted for a later flight going to Brisbane.

22 August, we departed Adelaide on Virgin 737-800 into Brisbane. Flight time back a quick 1hr 51mins. Sometimes from our home to/from Brisbane, we used a coach connection which offers door to door but on this occasion, we used

the train which comes from the airport through Brisbane to a station only 5 kms from our house. Brisbane airport is about 100 kms from us whereas Gold Coast airport is just about 20 kms. It's a good local airport if the schedules work!

A really good trip and great to meet up with Mike and Jill again. I didn't know I would see them again so soon!

Following day, the Sunday I put on my Care Flight Volunteer hat for an event being held right in Mudgeeraba, my home town. That was partly why we scheduled the flights to get back on the previous day.

Sad News from New Zealand

Then come the Monday, I get some very sad news from NZ that Marnie, in Tauranga, had passed away. She had died on the day we were doing the Murray River cruise.

We had both seen Ken and Marnie in November, the previous year on our motorhome trip up to Auckland, but Anne and her friend, Val, more recently had been on the Pacific Princess cruise in March earlier in the year, when it called in at Tauranga and Marnie had looked so well. She had been playing golf until mid-July!

Well regarding Marnie, you don't meet folks like this many times in your life. They had looked after us so well in the nine months we had stayed with them while we were building our house. It was without hesitation I decided at least one of us had to go over to NZ to attend her funeral and I departed two days later.

August to NZ

26 August, Departed Gold Coast on Air NZ Airbus A320 to Auckland flight time 2hrs 30mins.

I picked up a car and drove to Tauranga which is about a 2.5hrs' drive and found my B and B for the two-night stay. I met up with Ken and the rest of the family that evening.

Next day, I had the morning free and the funeral service was early afternoon just outside Tauranga, and I was honoured to be a pall bearer for the casket. I spent the evening with the family then back to my B and B. August 28th I headed to Auckland and went out to the NW area close to where we had built our house as this is where Mike and Jill still lived.

What a surprise to meet up with them less than a week after I had last seen them! You don't know what life is going to turn up! I spend the night with them and it was an afternoon flight next day, so we also had the following morning.

29 August, departed Auckland on Air NZ 767-300 to Brisbane with flight time 3hrs 28mins.

This 767 was delivered in 1995 so is now in its 20th year of flying.

I still speak with Ken and I think I've said before, we pick up the conversation like we ended the last one yesterday! That is uncanny but nice to know there are people like that around.

I found out earlier in 2021, his daughter was to be married later in October, and with the best will in the world I thought this Covid thing will be done and dusted by later in the year, and Anne and I could go over! It will be a phone call again!

December to Norway/UK

Anne's last long haul trip to UK was in 2008 and I don't think she is inclined to make any more. There are a few things on my 'bucket list' which involved northern climes, so Anne agreed I can head off on my own to Europe. My first sector from Brisbane to Bangkok was originally going to be a 777, but during the year Thai started to introduce the 787-800 series, so the equipment was changed shortly before my flight took place.

16 December, I departed Brisbane on Thai Airways 787-800 to Bangkok flight time of 8hrs 30mins (so, this is a new type see details below). Stayed overnight at an airport hotel but was taken there by Gene, a fellow traveller, from our Antarctic cruise. Many of us have kept in touch!

17 December, I departed in the morning on a Norwegian 787-800 (with Irish registration) enroute to Oslo flight time is a long 13hrs 4mins. This due to the downing of the MH flight over Eastern Ukraine the previous year, meaning we had to take a much longer precautionary route. Two years later, I flew the same airline, same sector in 10hrs 59mins, over 2hrs quicker.

One problem with 787's is that the window dimming can be controlled by the cabin staff as well as by the passenger's window controls. I've been trying for several times when on daylight flights flying alongside the Himalaya range to get good photos, but on this occasion, they had dimmed the windows without me realising and my photos have ended up with a blue caste to them, that I cannot photoshop out. Anyway, two years later, I made sure we get a good result!

I spent two nights in Oslo seeing a lot more of the city than on my previous short visit.

The Frogner park with all its sculptures in snow and mist in winter seems to have a much better appeal than seeing it in the summer.

I then travelled on train towards Bergen across the Norwegian plateau. In winter under deep snow this is just amazing! This was one on the list! I briefly stepped down onto the platform at Finse station which at 1222 m above sea level is the highest station north of the Alps.

Just further to the west, I changed trains at Myrdal and take the Flam railway down to the town on the fjord from where the rail gets its name. Normally in the summer, you would connect on to the Fjord steamer if you want to head to Bergen this way, but in winter it is mid-afternoon and close to sunset so there is little point as it will be dark very soon.

I stayed the night at the hotel on the Quay, and next day took the bus all the way to Bergen. Of the 170 kms or so to Bergen, I'd estimate nearly half was made up of tunnels! If there is a mountain in the way, they go straight through!

I spent two nights in Bergen and took a trip out to visit Edvard Grieg's house on the edge of a Fjord to the south of Bergen. I couldn't think of a better setting to compose music than the small music studio set down towards the water. I had been there before in 1968 and thought it worth a revisit.

It is now December 22nd, I departed Bergen on a BA Airbus A319 flight time to LHR 2hrs 12mins. There, I am met by my sister, Elaine, and her husband and enjoy Christmas and New Year with them and their extended family.

4 January, I'm headed north departing from Gatwick on Norwegian 737-800 (again with Irish registration) to Tromso in Northern Norway, flight time 3hrs 4mins. I had seven nights here, so main aim is to see the Northern lights which should happen on at least a few of the nights, in fact it happens on not less than five with two being really good displays!

Dogsled ride near Tromso northern Norway. January 2016.

I stayed at a small hostel type accommodation but had my own room, and they had their own minibus for the Aurora tours so that was way less than doing it with the bigger tour companies. On one day, I went out on a dog sled tour (see photo). I would much rather it had been on smooth sea ice. Going over normal terrain certainly brings up a few bruises on you at the end of the day!

Another day was the evasive Skidoo ride I had been trying to do for years. The idea was it was 90mins of riding with a changeover of drivers on a frozen lake at the turnaround point.

I rode the first 45mins and the last part of that was across a slope, so had to lean towards the mountain to keep the balance of the skidoo. The turnaround point on the frozen lake 850 m elevation about 15 kms from the Norway/Finnish/Swedish border junction temperature was -25°C! See the travel photo.

When Colin, my pillion rider, then took over the controls for the homeward journey, he couldn't seem to understand he had to lean towards the mountain to maintain us upright and despite me leaning as much as I could, and attempting to encourage him to do the same way, we ended up going downhill fast until we crashed, which was just as well, because there was a yawning gully a short way ahead!

Fortunately, no injuries resulted and he decided I had better drive the rest, so it was a fairly windy undulating track which took its toll on my arms and shoulders. By the time, I'd done 80mins of that, I had done a workout for the day. When I got home to Australia, I had a bit of a surprise. Most snow sports providing you are not in competition are included but I found Snow Mobiling was not covered!

Snowmobile ride again near Tromso northern Norway. January 2016

Sadly, on the first night out on the minibus on an Aurora tour I had been 20ft away from my Pentax camera on its tripod, when a freak gust of wind blew it over and destroyed it! One of my fellow travellers copied a few of his photos onto an SD card, and the one below is yours truly with the Aurora in the background.

Yours Truly with Aurora Borealis in background near
Tromso northern Norway. January 2016.

Now I should attempt to dispel a bit of a myth here about northern climes. Yes, it can be cold and as a Tromso bus driver said to me. "There's no such thing as bad weather, only bad clothing!"

You have all seen documentaries on Northern regions, especially Polar regions, and some talk about eight months of winter! We have two equinoxes' a year and every place in the world gets at least 12hrs of sun for six months of the year. In the arctic regions, it just happens to be more in the summer and less (or none) in the winter.

Having said that, let's just deal with a case where I have just been on this trip in Tromso which at just under 70 degrees north, is only a few degrees north of the Arctic circle which is around 66.5 degrees. This means over the northern Winter solstice December 22nd, the sun will not rise in Tromso, and in fact it doesn't actually rise there from November 27th, until January 15th, of the following year.

Now admittedly, it could be a lot gloomier on December 22nd than the photos I show, but the sun around midday is not far below the horizon plus with snow on the ground you do get quite a lot of workable 'daylight' around noon each day.

My daytrips out were at least a full week before the sun was due to reappear, but with all the snow around, it just seemed like a normal day and that would start from around 10 AM until at least gone 2 PM and then slowly get darker. I hope that might clarify some matters about daylight hours in arctic regions and a final tip about the clothing, always wear layers!

Oddly enough, despite Tromso's airport excellent setup for its winter operations and many air bridges for the many domestic flights that come and go for some strange reason International flights of which there are not many, passengers have to walk to the end of the finger, down stairs and brave whatever the weather might be doing to walk to their plane.

On the night, I left despite the bright lights of the apron on, as we walked across the snow, the Aurora was giving us a final display. A fellow guest from the hostel was on the same flight, and we were spending too long on the apron and had to be hustled onto the plane!

Again, at Tromso to aid in last minute de-icing their de-icing rigs are at each end of the runway for last minute application. That is a growing trend worldwide.

On January 11th, Depart Tromso on Norwegian 737-800 to London Gatwick, flight time 3hrs 11mins.

Hired a car and stayed at my sister's, then worked my way up the UK visiting friends and relatives. Some snow at this time, and didn't get to travel on some of the high Pennine and Lake District roads I had planned to, but finally arrived into Edinburgh where I saw King Penguins again at the Zoo there.

Paying my respects at the memorial to PA103 outside Lockerbie in Southern Scotland. January 2016.

I went to the Museum of Flight and went on my second Concorde, although sadly, have never flown on one. Many of my BA friends have flown long haul sectors on these planes but the best sector goes to my friend, Hedley, who I went to Bergen with back in the early days. They had a positioning flight so all BA staff could put their names in for a seat. So yes, Hedley has been on Concorde and he flew from Heathrow to Gatwick!

24 January, I departed Edinburgh on Easyjet Airbus A320 to Lisbon, flight time 2hrs 49mins

I had two nights here and stay in the old hilly quarter, just to the east of the city named Alfama, with its steep streets and cobbled alleys and trams. It is a delight to be there compared to all the modern cities that abound the world. I had paid a reasonable cost for an apartment that has river views of the Tagus river.

I had a great love of the national folk song called "Fado" and both evenings there, I went to small restaurants where a variety of singers accompanied by two guitarists, one which played the delightful Portuguese Guitar with its distinctive higher pitch.

My stay comes to an end too quickly and I returned up to UK for the last few days.

26 January, departed Lisbon on BA Airbus A320 to LHR, flight time 2hrs 51mins. Flight time is longer due a suspected French Air Traffic Control Dispute. The flight crew opt to take a flight up 9West longitude avoiding French airspace then fly in over Cornwall to LHR.

I had four remaining nights in UK spent with my family, then got taken down to Heathrow.

On January 30th, departed LHR on SQ Airbus A380 to Singapore, flight time 11hrs 59mins. This is a new type for me so see details below.

On Arrival, Singapore AM next day, connected onto same airline Airbus A330 to Brisbane, flight time 7hrs 13mins.

What an amazing trip!

I could note here that I am a tall person around 6ft 2inches and do not enjoy the rather cramped economy seating these days. I do wherever possible, pay extra money and it can be quite a small amount on a short European sector to pay for an exit row.

However, on long haul flights there must be many airlines who can cope with this request, but I have found Singapore airlines one of the most accommodating at finding me exit row seats on all the sectors I've used with them on the last two long haul trips. From Australia to UK, it adds around $360 to whatever economy fare you were paying. To my mind, that's a whole lot of value!

Boeing 787-8

Basically, a new generation of aircraft made of high strength composite materials with significant reductions in fuel burns and increase in efficiency. The 787 first took to the air on December 15th, 2009, and entered service with All Nippon two years later in October 2011.

It typically seats 242 passengers over a range of 7355 nmi. Later the -9 version took to the air and could carry 290. All Nippon experienced problems with the lithium-ion batteries on board, and 787's were grounded in 2013 from January to April while the problem was resolved.

As of June 2021, Boeing have built 1006 aircrafts. More recently the -10 model has been introduced, the launch airline being Singapore Airlines in April 2018 and some airlines plan to carry up to 330 on this model.

HS-TQE first flew on April 3rd, 2015 and delivered to Thai Airways on the 18th of the same month. My flight was later in the year on December 16th, 2015 from Brisbane to Bangkok.

Flight time was 8hrs 30mins. Have shown photo of aircraft prior to departure from Brisbane.

This aircraft has remained with Thai but has been parked since March 2020.

I have flown on three 787-8 sectors in total, the other two being on Norwegian from Bangkok to Oslo the first following on from this sector took a flight time of 13hrs 4mins due to avoiding east Ukraine airspace. The other Norwegian sector in October 2019 took only 10hrs 59mins being allowed to take a less onerous routing.

Boeing 787-8 December 2015. Prior departure from Brisbane.

Airbus A380-800

This aircraft sometimes termed the 'Superjumbo' having two full decks of passenger seating, has perhaps arrived at an unfortunate time in world history.

With the advent of Airbus's own A350 and Boeing's own 777 and 777X and 787 all coming into the market place, filling an A380 seems a bridge too far for most airlines, and it has to be very full to be economic.

Covid has since arrived on the scene in early 2020, and it could be some time before air travel returns to some degree of normality. In the meantime, most airlines are not flying their A380's or flying a reduced number. So far 248 have been built and three are yet to be delivered, and production ends in 2021.

The type first flew on April 27th, 2005 and entered service with SQ on October 25th, 2007. Typical seating of 525 is offered in three classes and a range of 8000 nmi can be achieved.

9V-SKI, the plane I flew on, was delivered to SQ in July 2009. My flight from LHR to Singapore was on January 30th, 2016 taking 11hrs 59mins. At that time, the aircraft was one of two painted in a colour scheme to reflect the airline's fiftieth year of operations. The colours were on the plane from May 2015 until June 2017.

SQ had some A380's in its fleet with economy seating at the rear of the upper deck and the daylight departure out of London which I was on, happened to be that type of seating, so I enjoyed a very quiet seat at the rear of the upper level and most certainly the quietest ride of my aviation travels. Photo used was taken at the LHR gate prior to departure.

This aircraft is now stored in Singapore as of March 21st, 2020.

Airbus A380-800 January 2016. Prior departure at LHR. This aircraft was one of two painted at the time in a scheme to celebrate SQ's fiftieth anniversary.

2016

Lifeflight

The new name for Care Flight, as they are now known, had a French themed night at the Brisbane hanger. I was not too involved now with the work as the flights were out of Brisbane airport, the maintenance was being done out at Archerfield airport the other side of the city. I had helped train up Brisbane locals to be new volunteers to be tour guides to show groups round that hanger on tours.

However, the French night needed all hands-on deck and my model needed TLC in moving from place to place, so I was anxious to be there. So, after the 200 diners had enjoyed their evening, at the end of the night, all the full-time staff had gone to a Brisbane hotel for a few hours' sleep.

One of the newest Helicopters, an Augusta Westland 139, had gone out on a rescue mission during the evening, but the two Lear jets were in the hanger, which is unusual because one is usually based up north in Townsville, so I became caretaker in the hanger for the night to the two Lear jets and the AW139 when it returned!

I certainly enjoyed my time as a volunteer. They do great work and are a great bunch of people! Photo I've shown is yours truly with Vicki and Chris from Lifeflight with the Lear jet model in French themed outfit. "VVI" on which it is based is the left hand aircraft in the background in later colours than when the model was built.

A French-themed gala dinner at Brisbane Airport marked the end of my time with Careflight/Lifeflight. Two staff, Chris on left and Vicki plus yours truly and the Lear jet model I made in the foreground. May 2016.

August to Cairns

As in years previous, flights from Gold coast to Cairns non-stop have operated and we have used them but there have been many years when none have operated. Jetstar are now on the scene running two flights per day, so we took advantage of at least a northbound one.

12 August, we departed Gold Coast on Jetstar Airbus A320 to Cairns, flight time 2hrs 5mins

We got a transfer up to Port Douglas for a two-night stay, meeting up with Mike and Jill from NZ who had been there already for a couple of days, and already have a rental car. We saw a little of Port Douglas the next day, which is a beautiful spot at the northern end of a great beach and the town is a jumping off point for many Barrier Reef trips.

After our stay, we head inland as the coastal road is in parts only 4WD but came back onto the coast at Cooktown for our two-night stay. This is as far north as you can go on the east coast of Australia.

Cooktown is famous for its Capt Cook history. His ship, the Endeavour, foundered on the Barrier reef not too far out in the Coral sea and he limped into the river mouth at what was to become Cooktown. The year was 1770 and everything is Endeavour here the reef, the River you name it. It took them seven weeks to make good repairs to the ship.

After our stay there, where the weather could have been kinder, we retraced our steps back south, but this time to spend our last two nights at Ellis Beach. You can't go past a good thing!

Finally, we were all headed out of Cairns airport on the same day, so we saw Mike and Jill off at the International terminal, then it's only a short walk to the Domestic for both of us.

This time it suited to take a flight to Brisbane.

On August 18th, departed from Cairns on Virgin 737-800 to Brisbane, flight time 1hr 53mins.

November Gold Coast Airport Ambassador Programme Starts

I saw advertised in our local press a new scheme at Gold Coast airport for an Ambassador scheme to assist passengers with any difficulty or needing help or directions. As my Lifeflight work had basically moved to Brisbane, I applied for a position and was one of the first 30 that started the programme. I really enjoyed the work being back at an airport in whatever role I could do.

Admittedly, I'd enjoyed my travel agency days but I'd put that second on my preferred list of where I would want to be! The first year was definitely the best as there was no fixed position to work, so you could roam the terminal, and almost every minute of your shift you could find somebody looking lost or feeling helpless to assist!

After a year, however, a fixed help desk got installed and as on one of the shifts I did, I worked on my own I had to occupy the desk, despite the fact I was aware there would be potentially lost people around the building that needed help! The programme then expanded with up to 70 volunteers, but I reduced to one shift where I shared with one other, so we could share roaming and desk duty.

That made it more palatable, but after my return in November 2019 from my Europe trip, I left the programme. I've included in a following pages photo showing me in middle of picture with Qantas Capt. Richard de Crespigny and his wife, Coral. He had arrived up from Sydney and I'd recognised him as he came through to claim his bags but couldn't put a name to the face.

Then a moment later, saw a Limo driver with his name on a display board. I said "I know who you are looking for" and got the driver's phone number. Eventually, they met up but Richard rang me from the Limo saying he was most impressed with what we do.

He was up to speak at our Convention centre but could he meet up with me when he checked in for his flight back to Sydney in two days' time. I said that I would be delighted and the photo is the result, and I have his autograph in the book he wrote which Anne had purchased for me!

The book is QF 32. You might recall shortly after A380's started flying QF32 had just taken off from Singapore when a turbine disc in number 2 engine on the inner left wing did devastating damage to overall controls and systems on the aircraft.

Fortunately, this was a check ride, so there was the help of five crew up front on this flight, to work through the huge amount of trouble shooting that needed to be coped with, and that took some time to work through. They safely got the aircraft back onto the ground at Singapore's Changi airport but with some 50 tons still overweight and unable to use full flaps, and therefore, a much higher landing speed around 168 kts was mentioned, they landed on the longest runway of 4000 m and had just about 300 m left!

Capt. de Crespigny was awarded the Member of the Order of Australia for significant service to the aviation industry.

Now you know something of the Ambassador programme and the people we aimed to assist. There have been quite a few stories over the three years! I'm proud to say, it's been a great pleasure to have met Richard and his wife, Coral. They are a great couple, and I am grateful to Richard for giving me some advice on publishing this book.

Reflects my time at Gold Coast airport with the Ambassador Programme. Shows Richard De Crespigny (Captain of QF32) on left and his wife, Coral. May 2017.

2017

Anne's Friend

When I returned from Europe in January 2016, Pauline, a friend of Anne's (she had been our neighbour at our first house for thirteen years), had been ill, and passed away in early February of that year. I was a co-executor of her will which turned out to be rather complex one, and meanwhile her house needed weekly maintenance and upkeep, so I had a very busy year.

Finally, things were all resolved by March of 2017 and I was able to go ahead and make bookings for a trip to the UK. My great niece, Ellen, one of my sister's granddaughters, was getting married in early June and my brother had already booked his travel to attend. I'm normally a great planner but my hands were tied until Pauline's estate was all finalised.

May to Europe

Initially, I planned to travel via Milan to see a little of Northern Italy before heading to London but booking relatively late, couldn't get the seats I was looking for, so went a few days earlier with flights into Rome, so the following itinerary was the result.

On May 22nd, departed Brisbane on an SQ Airbus A330-300 to Singapore, bit of a wait till early hours of 23rd, and then on an SQ 777-200 to Rome flight time on that sector 12hrs 10mins.

That gave me the afternoon and the next morning, so I saw the major sights including the first tour arrivals into the Vatican museum the next morning when it was empty and seeing the Sistine chapel. By afternoon of that day, I was headed down on a train south through Naples to Salerno and then a ferry along the Amalfi coast for a three-night stay in Amalfi.

On one of those days, I took a bus up to a village called Agrigento which is the start of a cliff walk called the 'Path of the Gods' which heads west and ends up above Positano, from where I returned to Amalfi by ferry. What a beautiful part of the world!

After my stay, it was back to Salerno station for a day of rail travel via Rome, stopping at Pisa for the usual photo propping up the tower and ending my journey at Manarola, the second port up of the five on the famed Cinque Terre Coast. I had three nights here and my first day, I planned to walk between two of the ports which I achieved.

There was some path work in progress, so the complete path from end to end was not possible but to walk most of it in one day, you would have to be incredibly fit. I'm fairly fit but not that good. Instead, I used the visitors card. I had to use the rail that connects all the ports and saw them all.

A really beautiful place to see!

On 30th, I departed Cinque Terre by rail heading north to Milan for a flight to London.

Departed from Milan (Linate) on Alitalia Embraer E190 (a new type see details below) and landed into London City airport (another airport I've always wanted to land at!).

Hired a car there and drove up to my sister's where my brother from NZ had arrived previously, and then a few days later moved up north for our great niece's wedding up in the Lake district.

The family all had a great time, and then my brother and I travelled the rest of the time together some of it back down south revisiting places we had been as youngsters.

But for the trip home, I had in mind to visit some places in the Benelux countries and fly home from Amsterdam. My father had been in the British Army in WW2, and had passed through Bruges in Belgium, so I had always wanted to visit there.

On June 21st, I departed St Pancras in London on a Eurostar train to Brussels and connected there to Bruges. Such a delightful city to see, where I had two nights.

Next day, I was on a day tour to see the WW1 battlefields and the war cemeteries in the Ypres area. This was a moving day which ended with the playing of the last post at the Menin gate at one entrance to the town of Ypres.

Photo following page.

Playing the last post at the Menin Gate at Ypres in Belgium. June 2017.

After my Bruges stay, I trained on to Amsterdam for a two-night stay. I did a canal cruise and walked around the city in the full day I had there.

On June 25th, I departed Amsterdam on an SQ Airbus A350 (a new type so see details below) to Singapore and connected onto same airlines Airbus A330-200 to Brisbane. A really great trip, and the first time I've made a trip to London and never been to Heathrow! Into London City and out on Eurostar!

Embraer E190

Embraer have become a leading manufacturer in the short to medium haul airliner market, and the E170 first flown in February 2002, became the fore runner of several developments to the 175, 190 and 195. The 170 entered service with LOT Polish Airlines March 17th, 2004, and it carried 72 passengers in four across the cabin seating.

Once the 190 arrived, it's stretched to accommodate 100 passengers in two classes or 124 in an all-economy version. Up to March 2021 Embraer had built 1596 of these E models.

EI-RNE is the E190 I flew on and registration shows it's an aircraft leased from a company registering their planes in Ireland. This is a common practice in the aviation industry, and my first Norwegian sector Bangkok to Oslo was in a similar registered plane.

The above E190 was delivered to Alitalia on April 23rd, 2012 and my flight was from Milan (Linate Airport) to London City Airport. Many more types of jet are now permitted into this airport than previously, when jets were limited to the Bae146. Flight time was 1hr 26mins.

Aircraft has been parked in Italy since January 2021.

Photo is of sister ship RNB which presented better for the camera prior to departure.

Embraer E190 May 2017. Sister ship at Milan (Linate) on departure date.

Airbus A350-900

Originally, intended to be a development of the A330 but then changed to a new model similar to Boeings 787 using carbon fibre-based materials which produced a lighter stronger airplane, with lower fuel burn and far better economics. The first A350 took to the air on June 14th, 2013 and entered service with Qatar on January 15th, 2015.

The 900-series can carry from 300 to 350 passengers over a range of 8100 nmi, and the 1000-series that has followed can carry 350 to 410 over 8700 nmi. As of June 2021, Airbus have built 436 A350 units.

9V-SMK was my first flight on an A350. It was delivered to SQ in February 2017.

I took my flight from Amsterdam to Singapore on June 25th, 2017. Flight time was 12hrs 4mins. Photo shown is at Amsterdam prior to departure.

This plane still in active service with SQ as at August 2021.

As well as above I've flown two more A350 sectors in 2019 also with SQ.

Airbus A350-900 June 2017. Prior to departure at Amsterdam.

2018

July Local Helicopter Flight

Stewart came over from NZ to celebrate his eightieth birthday, so we made a trip to a resort called Tangalooma on Moreton island, which is out to the east of Brisbane. Although, you can just make out the high-rises of the city about 30 kms away you could be in a tropical paradise. It is right on Brisbane's doorstep. Well the due date (28 July) came around so birthday boy, Anne and I went for a six-minute ride in a Robinson R44 helicopter around scenic points close to the resort area. My 4th ride in a chopper but a new type so please see the details below.

Robinson R44

This four-seater helicopter was a development from the company's earlier two-seater R22 model. It's a utility machine used in many work places. Very few are probably used in passenger work other than in industry.

The R44 first flew on March 31st, 1990 and went into service in February 1993. It is powered by a 245 hp Lycoming engine, and has a maximum range of 300 nmi and cruise speed is 109 kts.

It has been a popular seller and up to 2019, Robinson has produced 6331 units. In January 2000, an uprated engine and other improvements were made and a newer version named the Raven is now coming off the production line.

VH-FHK was built in 2006 and is still in service. They operate the passenger joy flights for the resort but they have a number of helicopters and do other duties doing inspection work for Power authorities etc.

Robinson R44 Tangalooma Resort July 2018. Taken on the day.

August to Sydney

In early August, I got news from Lynda, Joyce's daughter, down in Sydney that her husband, Alan, had passed away. He had been ill for some time so it had been expected.

Our families have been close, and I felt it was right to travel down and support Lynda, so travelled down for three nights.

Departed Gold coast on August 6th, on Virgin 737-800 to Sydney. Returned also on Virgin same type on August 9th, to Gold coast (in time for Anne's birthday).

2019

January to NZ

Stewart's wife, Brenda, had fallen ill quite suddenly late in 2018, so after a brief sickness, she passed away December 29th, 2018.

We needed to go over to NZ of course, but what works in our favour here, with two airports to fly out of (Brisbane and Gold Coast) and the choice of Auckland or Wellington in the North island to fly into, it gave us the choice of four routes to find reasonable fares to travel on.

Bearing in mind our travel was to be early New Year and most low cost seats had been sold a long time back, it was fortunate, it didn't cost us too much.

2 January, we departed Gold Coast on a Jetstar Airbus A320 to Wellington, where we picked up a car for around a five hour drive up to Hastings on the east coast in Hawkes Bay. We stayed at an Airbnb as my brother's place was full with his daughter staying from the UK etc. We fare welled Brenda.

I had been best man at their wedding fifty-six years ago! In the remaining time we were there, Anne caught up with some of Brenda's relatives out from the UK, who she hadn't seen recently, as her last trip over there had been back in 2008.

On January 8th, we had an early start back down to Wellington and departed on another Jetstar A320 back to the Gold Coast.

March

Now I'm grounded! From earlier in 2014 when they found the problem with the Aorta in my heart, each year they had been monitoring it and for each year it had been unchanged.

Mine had been stable but for the one year from 2018 to early 2019, it had gone up 5 mm which put it into the danger zone. Well, I didn't have too long to think about it! The heart surgeon said "See you next Wednesday!"

Come one week later, on March 14th, I was on the table but at least afterwards they did give me a recovery room with a great view of Gold Coast airport's runway! The op took a while to recover from, and it wasn't until start of July that I could say I was 100% again.

Meanwhile, I'd planned to go over to NZ and help Stewart tidy up his small farm to help him prepare it for sale. That trip would have been in April. Normally Virgin will give you a credit but charge some fees to delay flights but I guess 'Open heart' doesn't get mentioned every day so they gave me full credit which we used in 2020.

August to Western Australia

Yes, you guessed, for when I was in hospital we should also have been in Western Australia! However, most things were transferable to a later date (sadly the weather wasn't). It was pretty cool when we got there! We planned another Motorhome holiday, concentrating on the SW corner of WA.

On August 11th, we departed Gold Coast on a Jetstar Airbus A320 to Perth note the flight time of 5hrs 5mins.

We had four nights in Perth which included a day's cruise out to Rottnest island about 20 kms off the coast from Fremantle, where you can tour the island by hop on hop off bus and see delightful Quokkas which are like tiny Wallaby. Very cute! Perth is a beautiful city with some great parks.

After our stay there, we then picked up a full-sized motorhome for the next fifteen nights and did a circuit round the SW corner of WA seeing amazing Surf, limestone caves and beautiful scenery and trees that seem to reach for the sky! We need to return to see the top of WA! Our tour came to a close at the end when we dropped the motorhome at Perth Airport.

On August 30th, we departed Perth on a Jetstar Airbus A320 to Gold Coast flight time just 4hrs 2mins. Note the difference in flight times going west at over 5hrs to coming east at just over four. These are all factored in to airline schedules due to the prevailing winds, but that is one of the more extreme differences I've seen on a relatively short flight time.

October to Norway then Lower Europe

Well I was lucky. This was a well-timed trip bearing in mind what lay ahead in 2020!

I wanted to visit the Lofoten islands off the NW coast of Norway and get to sail on Hurtigruten's MV Lofoten. Both of these have been on my wish list since my Scandinavian trip in 1999!

On October 16th, I departed Brisbane on a Thai Airways 777-200 (they have changed back from 787's) and head to Bangkok. Flight time 8hrs 42 mins. Stayed at the same overnight airport hotel but this time Gene, my Antarctica friend, was not in town. I missed him by about ten days!

17 October, departed Bangkok on Norwegian 787-800 to Oslo, flight time, now a very quick, 10hrs 59mins. This time the cabin crew don't dim my windows whilst we passed the Himalaya Range around 3hrs after take-off, and I got some worthwhile photos! 4th time lucky! See photo which is around the Annapurna region and about 180 kms distant from the plane!

At fourth attempt! A reasonable image of the Himalayan range. This is somewhere in the Annapurna region, and distance from the aircraft around 180 kms. October 2019.

On arriving Oslo, stayed at an airport hotel overnight and returned next morning for onward flight to the Lofotens.

18 October, departed Oslo on Wideroe Dash 8 north to Leknes towards the Southern end of the Lofoten Islands, flight time 1hr 55mins. I had three nights

here in an apartment just outside the town, and next morning made an early start right down to the south of the island chain. There is some spectacular scenery here.

Unfortunately, returning up to Leknes and intending to do a few detours off the main road to see a few fishing villages, the road gets into the shade of a mountain range for 5mins or so, and side windows started to mist up, and fumbling around in an unfamiliar car to find the down buttons for the windows, my concentration on the road lapsed and the two nearside wheels ended in the ditch! See the photo of my attempt at parking a car in Norway!

Fortunately, Avis up at the airport didn't seem too fazed and were there in 45mins, pulled me out and thought nothing more of it. I did though. My confidence was really shot. I went gingerly back to the apartment and following day, only had a very limited excursion out. The night before though, we did get a good display of the Northern lights which cheered me up.

Not my best attempt at parking! The Lofoten Islands in Northern Norway. October 2019.

It was now time to drive north to the main capital of the Lofotens at Svolvaer, but sadly my stomach complaint that I had back in 2014 was back, so I spent most of my time in the capital in a doctor's surgery. The silver lining, if there was one is, it was raining outside so I wouldn't have been doing much sight-seeing!

On my departure from Svolvaer, I drove the car back south (about 3hrs) to a port called Stamsund. This is quite near Leknes so Avis can pick the car up from here. That evening, I departed on MV Lofoten a long-awaited trip. It is only an overnight up to Tromso where it arrives mid PM next afternoon.

This is how liners should look small and friendly. The photo shown was taken of it when we were passing it in 1999 on the Nordlys one of the more modern 11000 tonne ships. We briefly sighted the northern lights that evening before turning in.

On October 24th, after docking in Tromso, I headed to the airport and departed on a SAS 737-800 down to Oslo, flight time 1hr 42mins, again staying at an airport hotel.

25 October, I departed on a SAS Canadian Regional Jet CRJ900 to Aberdeen, again, a new type see details below. By this time, I'm feeling somewhat better with medication from the Norwegian doctor, and decide to go ahead with my hired car and itinerary down the west coast of Scotland.

I drove NW via Inverness to stay two nights near Applecross pass which I haven't visited since my winter trip of 1965. Now on the next full day, I revisited the Applecross area and arrived on the summit of the pass at lunch time, which I had with me in the car. The summit is very misty and pretty bleak (temp probably about +5C and windy).

MV Lofoten. After a 20 year wait I finally get to ride on this lovely old style Vessel. October 2019.

The photo I've shown is of three cyclists talking to one of the people from the motorhome. I couldn't resist talking to cyclists so went over and the female from the motorhome was asking the cyclists and me to come in for a cup of tea? I incorrectly assumed this might be the cyclists support vehicle and asked her but she didn't say NO!

A bogus support vehicle with 3 cyclists gathered around it at top of Applecross Pass one of the highest in UK at 2054ft October 2019.

The cyclists left and I went back to my car to have my lunch and tea. After that, I was curious as to how the support vehicle kept in touch with the cyclists, knocked on the door, was invited in made very welcome, then started to ask my questions then found out they were just touring around and weren't a support vehicle!

We all had a good laugh!

Then I headed south via the Isle of Skye to revisit Elgol which has magnificent views of the Black Cuillins across the water (see earlier photo January 1965). On way, back up the road to catch the ferry to the mainland I meet the cyclists again so have to stop and tell them yesterday's story!

I got back over on to the mainland at Mallaig on the only ferry that runs on a Sunday and stayed one night enroute heading south. I was planning to stay one night at a small hotel in Northumberland NP which is a 'Dark Sky' area but I cancelled it.

My health was playing up, so I added an extra night to my B and B stay near my cousin's house in SW Scotland and spent the following day at their local hospital. Eventually things settled down but in reality, whilst I enjoyed everything, I saw on this holiday although, it was of five weeks' duration, it really felt like ten weeks!

Overall, I had four nights staying near my cousin and this is an area where the "Hyslops" originated or at least our part of the family, so I often do some family research while I'm in the area and managed to achieve some worthwhile background information whilst I was there.

After that, I headed south and as winter hadn't set in was able to go over the Lake district roads and the Pennine hills that had evaded me before. So, in the usual way, I visited all the usual friends and relatives until I departed from my sisters in mid-November. November 14th, departed LHR on a Portuguese TAP Airbus A320NEO to Lisbon (a new type so please see details below).

I have three nights in Lisbon. Such a beautiful city! I booked a long time back and they have lost my booking in the system, but eventually gave me a river view apartment, not as great as previous but at fairly good rate, so I was happy. This stay gave me more time to look round, and first and third nights were spent at Fado evenings.

Also, Saturday morning was a flea market which was pretty big and full of interest. In my travels, I also found one of the outlooks I had been to in 1964 which is now very popular and people congregate there. There were ice cream trucks, buskers and wall to wall people! Back then, I was the only person there!

I've included a photo of one of Lisbon's famous trams. On the brow of a hill coming into Alfama, there is turn and coming over the hill plus the turn occasionally lifts a wheel of a tram off the rails. It is known as '3 Wheel Corner!'.

Lisbon Tram coming over the hill into Alfama district over the famed
'Three Wheeled Corner'. November 2019.

After an enjoyable stay in Lisbon, time to depart.

17 November, departed from Lisbon again on TAP on an Airbus A319 to Milan Malpensa airport, flight time 2hrs 23mins. I had a hire car (Fiat 500) but

it's night time, so made the decision to lose one night of the Lake Como stay, and spending it close to Malpensa airport, and do the rest of the journey first thing next morning.

Following morning, I arrived Bellagio after around a two-hour drive in some bright sun, and captured some photos on arrival but the sun didn't last long and it clouded in the rest of the day, so I walked around the town and saw Bellagio but not at its best.

Next day, it was raining but I took ferries to other parts of the lake and visited a market, but November isn't renowned for good weather here, but at least I have seen it!

I returned to Malpensa airport after the two-night stay.

20 November, I departed Milan Malpensa airport on SQ Airbus A350 to Singapore, flight time 11hrs 30mins.

And on November 21st, on daylight flight depart Singapore on another SQ A350 to Brisbane.

Well I'm glad I got to the Lofotens and sailed on MV Lofoten but Australia? Well it was good to be home from that one!

Bombardier CRJ900

The plant building this plane is based in Montreal (it was originally DeHavilland Canada) but Bombardier now have ownership. All the model numbers 550/700/900 and 1000 are derived from earlier aircraft from this manufacturer. The 700 took to the air on May 27th, 1999, and could carry up to 78 and the type went into service with Brit Air in 2001.

The 900 was a stretched version and can carry up to 90, and has a range of up to 1550 nmi. Bombardier have produced 924 and build of this type has now finished in 2021.

EI-FPR again, although, operated by SAS is a leased plane with an Irish based company. My flight was from Oslo to Aberdeen on October 25th, 2019 with flight time 1hr 20mins at 38000ft. Photo is prior to departure from Oslo's Gardermoen airport from an outer stand. This airplane is still with SAS although, was stored at Dublin from November 2020 to July 2021.

Bombardier CRJ900 October 2019. At outer stand prior to departure Oslo.

Airbus A320NEO

This has been mentioned before but Airbus wanted to improve on the existing version of the A320 which had been flying since 1987. A New Engine Option (NEO) was introduced plus many other major improvements to increase efficiency. The overall effect is to reduce fuel burn by around 15 to 20% compared to the original A320 and a greater range.

The other feature added which Airbus call 'sharklets' which many in the aviation world call winglets. However, some of the older models will get these updated modifications so the end of the wings won't always tell you are looking at a NEO! You might need to look at the engines as well, which are pretty distinctive.

First NEO took to the air on September 25th, 2014 and the type entered service with Lufthansa on January 25th, 2016. It's the same fuselage size as the 320, so passenger load remains the same at a maximum of 180 in a one class cabin.

The new engines that have made this possible are either the General Electric CFM Leap engine or the Pratt and Whitney 1000G.

CS-TVF was delivered to TAP Air Portugal in July 2019, and my flight was from LHR to Lisbon on November 14th, 2019. Flight time 2hrs 25mins.

This plane is operating in Star Alliance colour scheme same as my first A320 flight see June 2005. To repeat showing same colour scheme twice, I have shown below a sister ship A320NEO in the more normal TAP colours.

Airbus A320NEO November 2019. A pre-delivery photo showing French registration on the rear fuselage. Photo courtesy of EUROSPOT.

Doctor's Report

Well after that rather unfortunate health experience while travelling, I went to see my normal GP on my return, and an exploratory was organised which took place early in the new year, but things had settled down once more. I guess these things happen from time to time.

2020

February to NZ

My nephew, Mark, in Christchurch and his wife, Karen, were both turning fifty this year, so they decided to have a '100 Birthday Bash' the invite read: 'Come as a person you most admired or to reflect a period of time when you would have liked to have lived'.

Well my aviation options were to go as 'Sully' of "Miracle on the Hudson" fame, but that meant shaving my beard off! Or going as Abe Lincoln which after my Panam days, and the nickname that's followed me since, was really as they say, the no brainer!

I also needed to get my father's old carpenter's tool chest over there to Mark's and that would have had an extra bag charge on economy fares. As we needed Virgin only one way, the credits I had from the year before came in very handy because they virtually paid for one way in biz class for two fares. Yes, we paid a little more but for the first time in ages sat in 1A and 1C, and it didn't cost for the tool chest as we get two bags each in biz class!

16 February, an evening flight on Virgin 737-800 from Brisbane to Dunedin close to the bottom of the South Island of NZ, flight time 3hrs.

We had three nights there and due to late arrival picked up a car in town midday next day.

There was some revisiting of sights we had seen before, but on our second day, the morning was very foggy, so little was seen for that part.

When we left Dunedin, we had a few nights to get to Christchurch and we took an inland route to visit Mt Cook. Normally, you can do that as a day trip from a place called Twizel which is at the road leading into the Mt Cook valley, but accommodation there was heavily booked, so we stopped one night short of Twizel, then one night the other side after we had seen Mt Cook.

Finally, we arrived at Mark's which was the day before the party, and we picked up Stewart plus Gail, his daughter, and her partner, Trevor, both from the

UK who were all staying with us at an Airbnb booked for eight nights at a beach to the SE of Christchurch.

Next night was the party, and whilst there were no prizes for best dressed, Abe and Mary Todd Lincoln were up there with the best! See photo!

Towards the end of our stay, we spent two nights with Stewart up at Kaikoura and went out on a whale watch, then returned back down to Christchurch for our flight home this time back down to economy class!

2 February, departed Christchurch on Jetstar Airbus A320 to Gold Coast, flight time 3hrs 5mins

That was flight 454. Not sure how many more there will be.

Didn't realise Covid was only a matter of days away from stopping the world!

The fancy dress party in NZ. After my years with Panam and nickname of "Abe" it was a no brainer! A photo of Abe and Mary Todd Lincoln! February 2020.

Travel Trivia

I hope you have enjoyed reading my story and about the places I've been on my travels around the world. On reflection, I think it has been a fairly unique life. True, there would have been others with similar travel patterns but having worked for airlines for eighteen years and starting travel on my own before that, then following the airlines with twenty-four years in travel agency work, and continuing to travel into retirement, it has totalled fifty-nine years of air travel.

Looking back, I'm rather amazed at how many journeys I've achieved. Here are some of the statistics:

The flight sectors have totalled 454 which has encompassed 64 different types of aircraft.

Close to 50% have been on Boeing aircraft at a count of 225. In the Boeing count, 77 were 737's and coming a close second were 75 Boeing 747's which did include all series and the SP's and the freighter.

In terms of countries visited, it probably isn't a great number as it comes out at 43, as many of the routes I travelled tended to be the same visiting my brother down under from London to Auckland. I have, however, set down at numerous other places enroute. Other folks might put these in the count but I'll leave them out!

Somebody then asked me how many airlines had I flown on? So that totalled 50, plus there were three other operators running Cessna Floatplanes and the like.

Longest flight is not long by today's standards but it was Buenos Aires to Auckland on an Aerolineas A340 in 2007, and flight time was 13 hrs 17mins. Shortest flight was the Sikorksky S55 helicopter ride in 1963 at a whole 5mins, but the shortest scheduled flight was the Cessna 402 in the Hawaiian Islands, where the second sector was scheduled 15mins' blocks to blocks, but time in the air was just 10mins!

My shortest scheduled jet flight was on one of my SAS DC9 Stavanger to Bergen trips. Bergen is due north of Stavanger so with a northerly breeze if you take off on RW 36, and then fly due north and land on Bergens RW 36, we flew in a straight line for 16mins, whereas the normal blocks to blocks time is nearly double that at 30mins.

So, to leave on schedule and arrive 7mins early on a 99 mile sector is pretty impressive!

My fastest flight? It's difficult to decide because at a specific time one flight might be faster than another so overall one, has to take the distance between to two cities and the flight time, and come out with what hopefully is a fast or even record time for the sector!

My choice of quickest flights would be amongst four but I've chosen BOAC as the winner. A London–Bombay sector with Air Canada in January 1989 is one, another was SQ Singapore–Brisbane May 2004, and a third was Air NZ Auckland–LA in May 2005. All of these have been mentioned in the notes in the book. The top prize I think goes to the earliest which was a BOAC 707, May 10th, 1966 JFK-LHR with a flight time of 5hrs 47mins.

That gives it an average speed between the two cities of 597 mph! That involves riding a good Jetstream most of the way over the Atlantic and probably at times our speed over the earth was 700 mph! Sadly, in those days there were no display screens on the seat backs but in many cases since, I've been on flights and seen displays of 682 mph!

Now from my seat on the plane, I can record the time we depart the gate, our airborne and landing time and arrival time at the destination gate. All of this goes on to a small flight slip, which of course includes flight number, date, from/to etc. Also, usually when doors are just closing before start up, the flight deck come on the public address and Captain introduces himself, and often states the flight time and type of journey expected.

Sometimes I can get that information but on the longer trips, I give one of my old travel agency business cards to a cabin attendant and on the back, request the actual flight plan time, Captain's name (often these details are hard to hear on the announcement) and well into the journey ask them for the current cruise FL (Flight level).

The flight time from one slip purely gets transferred onto the next one to make up an accumulated total, and to date I have achieved just over 1427 flying hours, and I'm not going to tell you the actual time I've spent taxiing on the ground, but it's over FOUR days!

Glossary/General Information

AIR NZ (AIR NEW ZEALAND)
   New Zealand had two separate airlines, an overseas one called TEAL (Tasman Empire Airlines Limited) which operated until 1965, when it became rebranded AIR NEW ZEALAND. However, it continued to use TE flight prefix for its flight numbers until 1989 when NZNAC, the Domestic airline, was merged and Air NZ become both International and Domestic with an NZ flight prefix. See also NZNAC below.

ATC Air Traffic Control

BA British Airways from April 1st, 1974 (Combined BEA and BOAC)

BEA British European Airways until March 31st, 1974

BOAC British Overseas Airways Corporation until March 31st, 1974

BAC British Aircraft Corporation

BAe British Aerospace

CG Centre of Gravity

DEW (short for Dew line) Distant Early Warning station (stations positioned in Arctic regions from 1957 into the 1960s to warn North America of incoming attacks during the Cold war)

ESTA Electronic System for Travel Authorisation. Part of the USA visa waiver programme.

FAMIL Familiarisation Trips. These were either provided by an airline to show their aircraft being operated, or by a tour wholesaler to a destination to promote it to the travel agents on the famil.

FL Flight Level

HARS Historical Aircraft Restoration Society

HP Horse Power

LHR Heathrow

MD McDonnell Douglas

NEO New Engine Option

NP National Park

NZ New Zealand

NZNAC (New Zealand National Airways Corporation) commonly referred to as NAC and was the Domestic airline using NZ as its flight prefix until 1989 when it became absorbed into AIR NEW ZEALAND. (see above)

NMI nautical miles (or NM)

PPE Personal Protective Equipment

RAF Royal Air Force

RAAF Royal Australian Air Force

RJ Regional Jet (also prefix for Royal Jordanian Airlines but not used in this book)

RSPB Royal Society for Protection of Birds

RTOW Regulated Take Off Weight. For more see Flight planning in book year 1966.

RW (Runway) see also General Information below

SAA South African Airways

SAS Scandinavian Airlines System Founded in 1946 and is a consortium of airline cooperation among Sweden, Denmark and Norway.

SHP Shaft Horse Power

SKIDOO (Snowmobile is another name)

SOFIA Stratospheric Observatory for Infrared Astronomy

SQ Singapore Airlines

SR Short Range (note SR also was used as flight prefix for Swissair but the airline name is used in full in this book when applicable)

STA Scheduled Time of Arrival

STD Scheduled time of Departure

STOL Short Take Off and Landing

TCA Trans Canada airlines

TAA Trans Australia Airlines

TEAL See AIR NZ above

TOC Top of Climb. The point after take-off when a flight achieves its initial cruise altitude.

TOD Top of Descent The point at which the cruise ends and descent is initiated to land.

'TWOTTER' an affectionate name for Twin Otters! When I first flew on the type in the Solomons in Apr 1990 this was covered in the text.

TWA Trans World Airlines

UPS United Parcel Service
USAF United States Airforce
UTAG United Travel Agent Group
VHF Very High Frequency. In this context, refers to use of a radio transmission and navigation aids within the range of 108 to 137 Mega Hertz. The voice communication on set frequencies within that range is used between aircraft and ground such as Towers and approach controls, and is effective up to around 100 miles depending on altitude of the aircraft communicating as it is essentially dependent on line of sight.
VWP Visa Waiver Programme. Allows most visitors to enter the USA with relative ease for most short-term visits. Part of the programme involves obtaining and electronic online visa prior to entry (see ESTA)
747SP (Special Performance)

General Information

NON-STOP A flight operating from one point to another without stopping.

DIRECT FLIGHT (nothing to do with the above!) Buyer beware! This can be a flight with one flight number and have MULTIPLE STOPS! Detailed earlier in the book. G-ARWE, my flight took off on February 11th, 1968 and I mentioned before the routing was to Zurich then Beirut–Delhi–Rangoon–Hong Kong–Darwin–Sydney.

Believe it or not that flight from London to Sydney is called a DIRECT flight. So be wary what you ask for! Not many airlines stop as many times now, but a lot have flights with at least one stop, so each sector

Is NON-STOP but a flight with one flight number for example from A to C is direct! Some airlines get their terminology right, others do not and I think some take advantage of the average traveller's lack of knowledge. If you want Non-stop make sure that's what you ask for!

FIFTH FREEDOM This is one of the terms given to airlines allowed to carry revenue load between cities that are not in their own countries. As an example, in one of my early flights, I was able to board an Olympic airlines flight from Paris to London where the scheduled routing was from Athens via Paris to London. The ability to lift passengers from Paris to London as Olympic is not a French carrier is called a fifth freedom right.

Runway Directions

In some instances, in the book a runway has been mentioned such as 28L at Heathrow. This indicates the left of two runways at that airport with the other known as 28R (right)

The 28 indicates the approximate magnetic heading in tens of degrees i.e. 280, so slightly to the north of due west which is 270. If aircraft were operating towards the east due to the prevailing winds then the runways are then called 10L and 10R. All of these designators are painted in large numbers and letters on the threshold of each runway.

Now, just for an extra bit of information, things change over the years as the magnetic field in the earth's crust, somewhere up in northern Canada, is moving towards Siberia at around 30 miles per year! So, things start to change in the aviation world, and Heathrow amongst many other airports had to change its runway designators in 1987 and they are now 27 left and right, and of course, 09 left and right in the easterly direction.

May 2022: A Postscript

After a two year break due to COVID-19, the opportunity arose on the event of the author's 80th birthday for another flight!

A Trip in a vintage De Havilland DH82A beckoned, so seemed the obvious way of marking the event. My 65th type of aircraft and flight number 455. The photo was taken at RAF Duxford in UK in July 2008 of a similar DH82A.

The DH82 Tiger Moth was developed by De Havilland from their earlier DH60 Moth at Stag Lane aerodrome in NW London (oddly enough just over a mile from the author's birthplace.)

The DH82 first flew on 26th October, 1981, and entered service with the RAF in February 1932. It was designed as a primary trainer and many a military pilot and civilian ones cut their teeth by learning to fly on this type. Initially it was also used in the same role by the Royal Air Forces of Canada, Australia and

New Zealand. It was used right through until the 1950's when the De Havilland Chipmunk took over as a primary trainer.

The aircraft was powered by a De Havilland Gipsy 111 120HP engine, but when re-engined with the 'Gipsy Major' it became known as the 'DH82A'. I'm grateful to my friend from BA days, Stuart McKay, a member of Moth Club UK for providing his knowledge on this aircraft type.

In total 8,868 units were produced with initial production at Stag Lane but then moving to their main plant at Hatfield. It remained there until 1940 when it moved to Morris Motors at Cowley Oxford where close to 3500 units ended the UK production of this aircraft in 1944.

Index

This index is a slight variation on the normal one. Instead of page numbers you will find the month and year the trip started. The years have been included in larger characters and easy to find. As an example on our 2005 trip to North America the Airbus A320, a new type for me, was flown on the return in June but the reference will refer to May 2005 when the trip departed from Australia. Additional notes on some lines "+ photo" refers to the travel type photos which are also provided throughout the book for the readers interest.

Adelaide Aug 2015

Airbus A300B4-200 Sep 1997

Airbus A319-100 July 2008

Airbus A320-200 May 2005

Airbus A320NEO Nov 2019

Airbus A330-300 July 2008

Airbus A340-200 Nov 2007

Airbus A350-900 May 2017

Airbus A380-900 Dec 2015

Alaska May 2005 + two Photos

Ambassador, Nov 2016 + Photo

Amsterdam May 2017

Anvil cloud Aug 1974 + photo

Annular Eclipse Apr 2013 + photo

Antarctica Nov 2007 +four photos

Armstrong Whitworth Argosy AW650-200 Sep 1967

Athens July 1970

Austin 7 Jan 1971,Dec 1973 with photo

Avro 748-2A May 2005

BAC111-500 Feb 1969

Bae146-300 Mar 1992

Bali Mar 1992

Barra Airport Sep 1962, July 2008 inc photo

Belfast June 1962

Bangkok Sep 1996, Dec 2015,

Oct 2019

Bergen June 1968, July 1999,

Dec 2015

Boeing 707-465 Dec 1962

Boeing 720 May 1969

Boeing 727-100 May1969

Boeing 727-200 Jan 1969

Boeing 737-200 Aug 1980

Boeing 747-136 Oct 1973

Boeing 747-100F July 1978

Boeing 747SP July 1978

Boeing 747-200 June 1981

Boeing 747-238Combi June 1981

Boeing 747-300 Jan 1988

Boeing 747-400 Aug 1991

Boeing 757-200 May 2004

Boeing 767-200 Sep 1988

Boeing 777-200 Sep 2003

Boeing 787-8 Dec 2015

Bombardier CRJ900 Oct 2019

Brisbane Sep 1981

Britten-NormanBN-2 Islander

Dec 1987

Bruges May 2017 + photo

Buenos Aires Nov 2007

Cairns June 1994, July+Sep2003,

Nov 2012, Aug 2016

Canada Mar 1966, May2005 +photo

Canadair CL44J Mar 1966

Canberra Nov 1997

Capt Al Haynes Oct 1973

Capt Cliff Taylor Feb 1968

Capt Eric Moody Nov 1988

Capt Richard de Crespigny Nov 2016

Careflight Feb 2012 +photo

Cessna 172R Skyhawk May 2011

Cessna 185 Skywagon June 1968

Cessna 208B Grand Caravan   Mar 2011

Cessna 402A Aug 1980

Christchurch Dec 1990, Feb 2002,

Sep 2011, Feb 2020 +photo

Cinque Terre May 2017

Convair CV440 Metropolitan Aug 1968

Crete Oct 1972

De Havilland Comet 4B Mar 1961

De Havilland Dragon Rapide Jan 1964

De Havilland Heron 1B Sep 1962

De Havilland Canada DHC6 Twin Otter Apr 1990

De Havilland Canada DHC Dash8-200 Oct 2005

Denpasar Mar 1992

Douglas DC-7C June 1961

Douglas DC8-33 Jan 1969

Douglas DC9-40 June 1968

Douglas DC10-30 Oct 1973

Dornier 228 May 2004

Dunedin Sep 2011, Feb 2020

Embraer Bandeirante 110 Feb 2002

Embraer E190 May 2017

Falklands Nov 2007 +three photos

Faro July 1971, Apr 1972

Faroes May 2004 +one photo

Fokker Friendship F27 Feb 1968

Fokker F50 July 1999

Gibraltar Mar 1973

Glasgow Aug 1961, June+Sep 1962, Jan 1965, July 2008

Gold Coast QLD Apr 1980

Greenland Apr 1969 +two photos

Guanaco Nov 2007 + photo

Hamilton Island Apr 1987

Handley Page HP44 Dart Herald Sep 1962

Hawker Siddeley Trident 1C Mar 1966

Hawker Siddeley Tridet 2E July 1970

Hawker Siddeley Trident 3B Apr 1972

Helsinki July 1999, July 2008

Himalaya Oct 2019 +photo

Hong Kong Aug 1991, Sep 1995,

July 2008

Honolulu Aug 1979, Aug1980,

Oct 1981

Iceland May 2004

Innsbruck June 1965, Feb 1969

Inverness July 1973

Japan Oct 1990, Dec1994

Lady Elliott Island Dec 1987,

Mar 2011 +photo

Lake Como Oct 2019

Lifeflight May 2016+ photo

Lisbon Sep 1964, Dec 2015,

Oct 2019 +photo

Lockheed L1011 Tristar July 1976

Lofoten Islands July 1999,

Oct 2019 +photo

Longreach Oct 2005

Lord Howe Island Dec 2006 +photo

Los Angeles June 1981, Nov 1988

Macau Sep 1995

McDonnell Douglas MD80 Jul 1999

Melbourne Sep 1981, Dec 1992, Jan 2004

Milan Sep 1967, May 2017

Nandi Feb 1990

Napier Feb 1968, Oct 1996

New York Mar 1966, July 1976

New Zealand Feb 1968, May 1969,

Jan 1971, Oct 1973, Aug 1974,

Dec 1990, Oct 1994 , Mar 1997,

Nov 2009, Sep 2011, Nov2014,

Aug 2015, Jan2019, Feb 2020

+3 photos

North America Mar 1966,

May 2005 + photos

Northern Territory Apr 2013 + two photos

Noumea May 1994, Apr 1995

Oslo July 1999, Dec 2015,

Oct 2019.

Orkney Islands July 2008

Paris June 1961, Jun1963, Jun1965,

July 1971

Patagonia Nov 2007 +photos

Perth Aug 2019

Recumbent Nov 1997 +photo

Rio De Janeiro Jan 1969 +photo

Robinson R44 July 2018

Rome May 2017

SAAB 340A Oct 1994

Santiago Jan 1969

Scandinavia June 1968, July 1999,

Dec 2015, Oct 2019 + photos

Scilly Isles Jan 1964

Scotland Jun 1962, Jan 1965,

July 1973, July 1999, May 2004,

July 2008, Dec 2015 ,Oct 2019,

inc four photos

Shetland Islands July 2008

Sikorksky S55 May 1963

Sikorksky S61N Apr 1969

Singapore Dec 1988, Sep 1997,

Sep 2003

Solomons Mar 1990 + photo

South America Jan 1969, Nov 2007 + photos

Spitzbergen July 1999 + photos

Stockholm Apr 1968, July 1999

SUD AVIATION Caravelle III June 1963

Switzerland June 1961, June 1965

Sydney Feb 1968, Jan 1971,

Oct 1973, July 1978, Mar 1979, Apr1980,

Mar 1981, Feb 1982, (since then many trips to Sydney

per my note in "Sectors" at front of book.

Tahiti Dec 1976

Tanglooma July 2018

Tangier (via Gib) Mar 1973

Tasmania Nov 1995, Feb 1999

Torres Del Paine Nov 2007 +photos

Tromso July 1999, Dec 2015, Oct 2019

UK July 1976, Aug 1979,

June 1981,Jan +Nov 1988,

July 1999,May 2004,

July 2008 ,Dec 2015,

May 2017, Oct 2019 + photos

USA Mar 1966, May 2005 + photos

Ushuaia Nov 2007

Vanuatu Mar 1994

Vickers Vanguard V953 Aug 1961

Vickers Viscount V802 Mar 1961

Vickers Armstrong VC10 Aug 1974

Vickers Armstrong Super VC10 Feb 1968

Western Isles July 2008 + photo